HYPERTALK
INSTANT
REFERENCE

The SYBEX Prompter™ Series

HYPERTALK™ INSTANT REFERENCE

Greg Harvey

San Francisco · Paris · Düsseldorf · London

The SYBEX Prompter Series
Editor in Chief: Rudolph S. Langer
Managing Editor: Barbara Gordon
Series Editor: James A. Compton
Editor: Tanya Kucak

Cover design by Thomas Ingalls + Associates

Apple, AppleTalk, Finder, HyperCard, HyperTalk, ImageWriter, LaserWriter, Mac,
Macintosh, MultiFinder, and Stackware are trademarks of Apple Computer.
dBASE Mac is a trademark of Ashton-Tate.
Excel, MS, and Word are trademarks of Microsoft Corporation.
MacDraw, MacPaint, and MacWrite are trademarks of Claris.

SYBEX is a registered trademark and Prompter Series is a trademark of SYBEX, Inc.

SYBEX is not affiliated with any manufacturer.

Every effort has been made to supply complete and accurate information. However,
SYBEX assumes no responsibility for its use, nor for any infringements of patents or
other rights of third parties which would result.

Library of Congress Card Number: 88-61069
ISBN 0-89588-530-1
Printed by Haddon Craftsmen
Manufactured in the United States of America
10 9 8 7 6 5 4 3 2 1

The SYBEX Prompter Series

We've designed the SYBEX Prompter Series to meet the evolving needs of software users, who want essential information presented in an accessible format. Our best authors have distilled their expertise into compact *Instant Reference* books you can use to look up the precise use of any command—its syntax, available options, and operation. More than just summaries, these books also provide realistic examples and insights into effective usage drawn from our authors' wealth of experience.

The SYBEX Prompter Series also includes these titles:

Acknowledgments

Thanks are in order to the excellent SYBEX team who made this book come into being:

Dr. Rudolph S. Langer, editor-in-chief
Dianne King, acquisitions editor
Jim Compton, Prompter Series editor
Jeff Green, technical editor
Jonathan Rinzler, proofreader
Cheryl Vega, typesetter
Jocelyn Reynolds and Bob Myren, word processors
Ingrid Owen, series designer
Evelyn Ong Sy, layout

In addition, I want to express a special thanks to Tanya Kucak, my copy editor, who did (and always does) her job with such care and finesse.

Table of Contents

Chapter 3

The HyperTalk Functions   142

Chapter 4
Properties in HyperTalk   229

Chapter 5
Constants in HyperTalk

Introduction

The *HyperTalk Instant Reference* provides a quick reference to all of the functions of HyperTalk. Although the *HyperCard User's Guide* provides an excellent introduction to creating and working with HyperCard stacks, it is almost totally silent about the rich and complex capabilities of HyperTalk. At present, your only source of information on HyperTalk is confined to the sections on HyperTalk in the Help stack included with the software. Although the information in the Help stack on scripting is helpful, it too falls short of giving you a complete reference to the commands, functions, properties, and constants included in the language.

This book is meant to fill in the gaps between the user's guide and the HyperCard Help stack. It assumes that you are familiar with the basics of using HyperCard to create and maintain stacks. However, it does not presuppose any programming experience, either with HyperTalk or with any other programming language.

Using the HyperTalk Instant Reference

This book is divided into five chapters to make it easy to locate the specific information about HyperTalk that you need. **Chapter 1** gives you an overview of HyperTalk. Look to this chapter if you need general information about writing scripts. You will also find information there on the HyperTalk control structures, including the If...Then, Repeat, and Exit constructions.

Chapter 2 contains a listing of all of the HyperTalk commands. This section provides you with reference entries for these commands arranged in alphabetical order. Each reference entry includes a brief description of the command's function, the form (or forms) it takes, arguments, usage, examples, and any special notes. At the beginning of this chapter, you will find a table organizing the commands into categories. This table also gives you the syntax of the command.

Chapter 3 presents the HyperTalk functions. The reference entries in this chapter follow closely those for the HyperTalk commands in Chapter 2. The functions are listed in alphabetical order and include a short description, form(s) of the function, explanation of its arguments, usage, and any special notes. At the start of this chapter, you will find a table that categorizes the functions and lists their syntax.

Chapter 4 gives you a listing of the properties in HyperTalk. Because properties are identified with the HyperCard objects they describe, you will find these entries segregated according to the hierarchy of objects. Within each group, the references are listed in alphabetical order. Each property reference includes a description of its function, usage, and examples. At the beginning of this chapter, you will find a table that organizes all of the HyperCard properties by object.

Chapter 5 lists the constants in HyperTalk. This list of reference entries is in alphabetical order. Each entry contains a brief description of the constant followed by an explanation of how it is used in HyperTalk scripts.

Programming Conventions Used in This Book

The programming conventions used in this book follow those used in the HyperCard Help stack. If you have used other programming languages, they are probably familiar to you. If you have not, you should take a moment to read over the following sections on how command and function arguments are noted. This will help you a great deal when you begin to use the reference entries for HyperTalk commands and functions found throughout the book.

Variable Arguments

All variable arguments are enclosed in a pair of angle brackets (as in <*file name*>). Within these brackets, you will find a term that characterizes the type of information required by the command. For example, you can state the argument for the Go command as

go <destination>

Because of the angle brackets, you know that an argument describing the destination is required by the Go command in order for it to work (you cannot just enter *go* without telling the program where to go).

In place of <*destination*>, you can enter many specific destinations, such as

go home

or

go last

or even

go to card 12 of stack "Stack Ideas"

Optional Command Words

The last example points up another consideration in entering HyperTalk commands. Its developers wanted to make HyperTalk as English-like as possible, so you can often enter prepositions as part of the command statement. Prepositions are not required for the program to execute the command correctly, however. The preposition *to* in the *go to card* command in the previous example is an optional command word. You can add or omit *to* as you wish when using the Go command. All optional command words are noted by enclosing them in a pair of square brackets ([*for*]). Therefore, the complete notation for the Go command is really

go [to] <destination>

Another example is the Wait command. This command pauses the program for a specified time or until a particular condition is met. It has several generalized forms:

wait [for] <number of ticks>
wait [for] <number> **seconds**
wait until <true or false expression>
wait while <true or false expression>

When you want the program to wait a specific number of ticks (60ths of a second) or seconds, the word *for* is optional. You can enter

wait for 5 seconds

or

wait 5 seconds

Either form instructs the program to wait 5 seconds before it continues to execute subsequent commands in a script. However, if you use the Wait command to have the program pause until a particular condition exists, as with *wait until* or *wait while*, the command words *until* and *while* are not optional.

Optional Arguments

Some commands have optional arguments that, if used, have additional required command words. The Open command is a good example of this type of command:

open [<document> with] <application>

This command can be used to start an application program with or without a particular document. For example, you can have Hyper-Card start Microsoft Word by entering

open microsoft word

However, if you want to start Word with a particular document file, you must enter the document's name and use the preposition *with* in the command:

open "Billing Statement" with microsoft word

If you choose to use an optional parameter that is enclosed in square brackets, you must enter all of the required arguments within the brackets for the command to work properly.

Alternate Arguments

A few HyperTalk commands have alternate arguments that you choose from when using the command. Alternate arguments are separated by vertical bars. For instance, the Put command contains such alternate arguments:

put <**source**> **before** | **into** | **after** <**destination**>

You can use the Put command to place the current date into a date field, as in

put the date into field "Today's Date"

You can also use it with the preposition *before* or *after* to locate field information in a particular order, as in

put field "City" before field "State"

When you are presented with alternate arguments, you must use one of the words separated by vertical bars when you enter the command into a script, unless the alternate arguments are enclosed in square brackets. For example, the Push command has two alternate and optional arguments:

push [this | **recent] card**

If you use the truncated form

push card

it means *push [this] card.*

Arguments of Functions

The notation system used to designate the arguments of commands is used in a similar manner to designate the arguments of a function. Some HyperTalk functions do not require any arguments at all, such as the Date and the Time functions. However, those functions that do require arguments use the same notation conventions as command arguments. Therefore, variable arguments are enclosed in angle brackets, optional parameters in square brackets, and alternate options are separated by vertical bars.

For example, the Number function has two forms that illustrate this clearly. You can use this function to have the program calculate the number of cards, buttons, or fields in a stack. When used in this way, the form is

the number of cards | **buttons** | **fields**

For instance, you could create a script that determined the number of cards remaining after you deleted a card with the Delete Card option on the Edit menu:

```
on doMenu Delete Card
   put the number of cards – 1 into the message box
end doMenu
```

You can also use this function to obtain the count of particular items (components) in a text field. When used in this fashion, the function has a slightly different form:

the number of <components> in <container>

Here, there are no alternate arguments. You must designate the items (*<components>*) you want counted and the field (*<container>*) that contains them. For example, you can use this form of the Number function to find out how many characters are in a particular text field:

the number of chars in field "Address"

When a HyperTalk function requires only one argument, you can choose either of two ways to enter the argument. For instance, you can enter the square root function, which calculates the square root of a number, either as

sqrt(<number>)

or

the sqrt of <number>

because it only requires a single number as an argument.

You can add a space between the function name and the argument enclosed in the pair of parentheses, if you wish. The program will accept

sqrt(49)

or

sqrt (49)

When a function requires multiple arguments, however, you must enclose the arguments in parentheses. For example, to calculate the average of a list of numbers, the Average function follows the general form

average(<number list>)

Therefore, to find the average of the numbers 12, 20, and 15, you have to enter it as

average(12,20,15)

You cannot enter

the average of 12,20,15

into your script.

CHAPTER 1

Writing Scripts in HyperTalk

HyperTalk is an object-oriented programming language included in HyperCard. With it, you can greatly expand the features and functions of the stacks you create in HyperCard. The language uses an English-like syntax, and it includes a complete command vocabulary (see Chapter 2). In addition, the language enables you to make use of a wide variety of built-in functions (see Chapter 3).

Procedures written in HyperTalk are referred to as *scripts*. HyperTalk scripts cannot stand alone; they must be attached to a particular HyperCard object such as the stack, background, card, field, or button. The scripts that you create for HyperCard objects allow them to communicate with each other and with the HyperCard program. When a script is executed, it sends and receives messages that permit this intercommunication.

Message Handlers

Each script message is sent and received by a *message handler*. All message handlers in HyperTalk begin with On followed by the name of the message and are terminated with End followed once more by the name of the message. For example, consider the following simple script that uses the most common message handler:

```
on mouseUp
  go home
end mouseUp
```

In this example, the entire script is the message handler for the MouseUp message. The On MouseUp message means "as soon as you (that is, the object that the script is written for) receive a MouseUp message, do the commands that follow." As such, it determines when the HyperTalk commands included in the message handler are executed. In this example, this is as soon as the object that contains this script *traps* (that is, intercepts) a MouseUp message—a message sent by HyperCard whenever the mouse button is released.

The End MouseUp message indicates the end of the message handler. Sandwiched between the On MouseUp and End MouseUp are the HyperTalk commands that are to be executed. In this example, there is only one HyperTalk command (*go home*) to be executed. When there are multiple commands, they are entered in the sequence they are to be executed. They are always placed between the On and End statements for the message whose interception initiates their execution.

A HyperCard object can be both the sender and receiver of a message. To be a receiver (referred to as the *target*), it must contain a matching message handler. To be a sender, it must contain Hyper-Talk commands whose execution causes HyperCard to generate a system message. Many times, this occurs in the same message handler, although a script can contain multiple message handlers, depending upon the events that could occur and that you want to control.

System Messages

The MouseUp message trapped by the On MouseUp...End MouseUp message handler is an example of a *system message*—that is, one sent by the HyperCard program when a certain event takes place. HyperCard is constantly sending system messages of one type or another. Even when no special event is taking place, it sends an Idle message.

You can see a list of all the system messages sent by HyperCard to various objects in Table 1.1 (also reproduced on the back inside cover of this book). This table arranges the system messages by the HyperCard object that receives and potentially traps the message (if the object has a script that contains the proper message handler). Notice that many of the system messages generated by the use of the mouse are sent to multiple HyperCard objects, including cards, fields, and buttons.

The Hierarchy of Objects

Even when a system message, such as the MouseUp message, is sent to several different HyperCard objects, it reaches each object according to its placement in the hierarchy of objects. This hierarchy of objects determines the way messages are *inherited* (or passed up the order), so it is also referred to as the message inheritance hierarchy. Figure 1.1 (also reproduced on the front inside cover of this book) describes the path of message inheritance laid down by the hierarchy of HyperCard objects.

When HyperCard sends a system message, the program searches for a matching message handler according to this hierarchy. For example, when the mouse button is depressed, this event causes a MouseDown message to be sent by HyperCard. The MouseDown message goes first to the object at the highest (closest) layer that the Browse tool is on. If this were a card button, the MouseDown message would be sent to this button. If a matching On Mouse-Down...End MouseDown handler is not found and thereby trapped by the script attached to this object, the message is passed to any button or field located on lower (farther) layers beneath it.

	To Card	To Field	To Button
Create	newCard	newField	newButton
	newBackground		
	newStack		
Delete	deleteCard	deleteField	deleteButton
	deleteBackground		
	deleteStack		
Open	openCard	openField	
	openBackground		
	openStack		
Mouse	mouseUp	mouseUp	mouseUp
	mouseDown	mouseDown	mouseDown
	mouseStillDown	mouseStillDown	mouseStillDown
		mouseEnter	mouseEnter
		mouseWithin	mouseWithin
		mouseLeave	mouseLeave
Key	returnKey		
	enterKey		
	tabKey		
	arrowKey		
Startup/	startup		
Quit	suspend		
	resume		
	quit		
General	help		
	idle		
	doMenu		

Table 1.1: System Messages Arranged by Function and Object

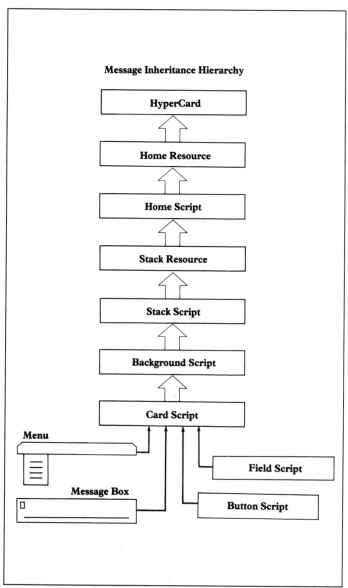

Figure 1.1: Message inheritance hierarchy

If there are no buttons or fields or they do not contain the appropriate handler, the message then continues up to the next highest object in the hierarchy. This passing of the message continues until an appropriate message handler is located in the script of an object, or until the end of the hierarchy (HyperCard itself) is reached.

Notice in Figure 1.1 that after passing the message from the card to the background script, it is passed to any stack resource that may be attached to that stack. This allows you to enter command statements that are not in the HyperTalk vocabulary but are meaningful to the attached resource (refer to the Play command in Chapter 2 for more information on this). After checking for any external resource attached to the stack, the message is passed up to the Home stack and, if necessary, to any resource attached to the Home stack. If a matching handler is not found by then, the message is finally passed to the program itself. If it cannot be handled, the system generates an error message telling you it has never heard of the message.

When creating HyperTalk scripts, you need to be aware of the hierarchy of objects, for it can help you determine where you place the script that traps for system messages. Each level up on the hierarchy is more general (that is, inclusive) than the one below it; it not only includes itself, but also all of the objects on the levels below it. For example, if you create a routine that should be globally available within all stacks, you attach its script to the Home Card stack. If you want the routine to be globally available within a particular stack, you need to attach its script to that stack or its background. If you want to restrict the routine to a particular card, you need to attach its script to the card, and so on.

Extending the HyperTalk Message Vocabulary

You are not restricted to using message handlers that trap only for the system messages generated by HyperCard. Indeed, one of the ways you can extend the HyperTalk message vocabulary is to create your own messages as part of the appropriate handlers to trap them. To create a user-defined message, you simply create the handler that contains the name you assign to the message. A user-defined message can also contain any parameters that further define its use. Such parameters are listed after the message name, separated by commas.

For example, suppose you want to be able to copy text from any stack that you are working with into an all-purpose reference stack, and then return to the card you were viewing as soon as the copy is made. You can do this efficiently by creating your own user-defined message as part of the message handler attached to the Home stack.

Assume that you call this message CopyDown. The On Copy-Down...End CopyDown message handler in the Home stack could contain the script shown in Figure 1.2.

```
on copyDown textString, copyField
    if textString is empty and copyField is empty then
        get selection
        if it is empty then exit copyDown
        else
            push card
            go to stack "References"
            doMenu "New Card"
            put it into field 1
            pop card
        end if
    else
        push card
        go to stack "References"
        doMenu "New Card"
        put textString into field copyField
        pop card
    end if
end copyDown
```

Figure 1.2: The CopyDown message handler script

In this example, the name of the message handler, CopyDown, is followed by two parameters: TextString, which can contain the text to be copied, and CopyField, which designates the name or ID of the field it is to be copied into.

After adding this message handler to the Home stack, you can copy selected portions of text from any card in any stack that you are working with. Because of the way the message handler script is set up, you can perform the copy operation in one of two ways. You can create a background button in the stack you are in whose script contains

on mouseUp
  copyDown
end mouseUp

In this case, you have only to highlight the text to be copied and then click this button.

Alternately, you can type the text into the Message box. In this case, you enter *copyDown* followed by the text you want copied and the name of the field it is to be copied into in the Message box. For example, to enter "King George I" into a field in the Reference stack named Monarchs, you would enter

copyDown "King George I", Monarchs

directly into the Message box. When using the Message box, the text *King George I* is used as the TextString parameter and *Monarchs* as the CopyField parameter, directing the program what to copy and where to copy it.

Using the Script Editor

Scripts are written with the Script Editor. You can access this editor by taking the following steps:

1. Set the user level to Scripting on the User Preferences card in the Home stack.
2. Select the appropriate Object tool—either the Browse, Button, or Field tool—on the Tools menu.
3. Select the HyperCard object you want to write a script for by selecting the appropriate Info option on the Objects menu.
4. Click on the Script button in the dialog box.

You can also go directly to the Script Editor to write or edit a script for a particular field by selecting the Field tool and then selecting the particular field by holding down the Shift key as you double-click on it. You can use this same technique to write or edit a button script, this time selecting the Button tool before holding down the Shift key and double-clicking on the appropriate button.

The Script Editor contains a scroll box in which you write and edit the selected object's script. At the top of the Script Editor window, the program identifies the object that the script is being written for (by ID and name, if assigned).

You enter and edit the text in the Script Editor as you do text in HyperCard fields. However, keep in mind that you only have access to the Cut, Copy, and Paste commands through their keyboard equivalents: Command-X, Command-C, and Command-V, respectively.

When entering the command statements of the script, keep in mind the following guidelines:

- Each group of HyperTalk commands must be sandwiched between a message handler.

- Each HyperTalk command statement is terminated by a carriage return (entered with the Return key, not the Enter key).

- Whenever a command statement requires the use of more than a single line, terminate the line with a soft carriage return (entered by pressing Option-Return and shown in the script by ¬).

- Each message handler begins with the word *on* followed by the name of the message and is terminated by its own carriage return.

- Each message handler ends with the word *end* followed by the name of the message and is terminated by its own carriage return.

Button Scripts

When you create a button script, HyperCard automatically enters the On MouseUp and End MouseUp statements for you and indents the flashing text insertion pointer one tab stop on a blank line between them. Because this is by far the most common message handler used in a button script, it allows you to get right down to entering the HyperTalk comands that you want executed when the Browse tool is located on this button and the mouse button is released. To use a different message handler, simply highlight *mouseUp* and type in the name of the message you want to use.

When creating scripts for any of the other HyperCard objects, the program makes no assumptions about the message handler you wish to use, and you must manually enter both the On and End message statements as well as all the HyperTalk commands to be executed.

Levels of Indentation

The Script Editor automatically indents portions of the script as you write it. It indents all command statements that are sandwiched between paired commands—that is, commands that must contain an open and close statement—by one tab stop. These commands include the On and End message statements of the message handler, as well as If and End If, and Repeat and End Repeat, statements. This method for setting off related groups of commands in the code is quite common in programming. However, whereas such formatting is done manually and its use is purely optional in other programming languages, it is built into the Script Editor, and its use in HyperTalk is therefore mandatory.

For example, whenever you enter On MouseUp in the Script Editor and press the Return key, the Script Editor puts in a carriage return and positions the cursor at the first tab stop on the next blank line. As you enter the command statements for that message handler, terminating each one with a Return, the cursor continues to be indented the same amount on each succeeding line. However, as soon as you enter the End MouseUp statement and press Return, the End MouseUp statement is automatically outdented so that it is positioned flush with the left margin and is in line with the On MouseUp statement above it.

The same type of indenting and outdenting goes on when you use an If..Then or Repeat statement terminated by an End If or End Repeat statement. The only difference is that you can nest these types of constructions, which inserts more levels of indentation into the format of the script.

When entering a corresponding End statement for a message handler or an If...Then or Repeat construction, you may find that the Script Editor does not automatically outdent the End statement to the same level as the first statement. If this happens, the End statement contains some kind of error. Most of the time with message handlers, you will find that you have made a typing error when entering the message name (it must match the name used in the On message statement). In the case of End If and End Repeat statements, the trouble is usually related to nesting—you should check to make sure that all earlier If...Then and Repeat constructions in the message handler are properly paired.

Locating Text in the Script

At the bottom of the Script Editor window are four buttons: Find, Print, OK, and Cancel. The Find button enables you to locate specific text in a script. This is useful if the script extends beyond the single window. Its use alleviates the need to scan each line as you scroll the text with the Scroll box to find the commands that require editing.

When you click on the Find button (or press Command-F), a dialog box appears in which you enter the text to be searched for. After entering the search string (text) and clicking on the Find button in this dialog box or pressing Return (or Enter), the program will highlight the first occurrence of the search string in the script. If it cannot locate the string in the script, you will hear the Alert Sound that you have set for your Macintosh.

Printing the Text of a Script

You can print the text of a script by clicking on the Print button (or by pressing Command-P). If you want to print only a part of the script, you need to highlight the text before you send it to the printer. The printout of the script contains a header showing the current date and time and identifying the object whose script it is.

Saving the Script

Once you have entered the text of a new script or edited an existing script, you will want to save it by clicking on the OK button. To abandon any modifications you have made to a script, you click on the Cancel button. If you press the Enter key (as opposed to the Return key), HyperCard responds by saving your script and returning you to the card level.

Once a script has been created and saved for a particular object, you can edit it at any time by selecting the appropriate Object tool, then selecting the correct Info option on the Objects menu and, finally, clicking on the Script button. You can also use the Edit Script HyperTalk command to go directly to the script of a particular HyperCard object to make your editing changes (see Chapter 2).

Debugging Scripts

If HyperCard encounters a command statement that it cannot execute while testing the script that you created, you will receive a dialog box containing an error message pointing to the problem. Along with the message, this dialog box contains two buttons: Script and Cancel. If you click on the Script button, HyperCard will take you directly to the Script Editor, and the cursor will be positioned at the place in the script that HyperCard could not interpret and execute. It is then up to you to pinpoint the error, make the correction(s), and retest the script (after saving it again). Note that HyperTalk does not contain any of the traditional debugging aids, such a step mode, control of the speed of execution, or a command log or history.

If you select the Cancel button in the Error Message dialog box, HyperCard will abort execution of the script and return you to the card. Then, to make your corrections to the script, you have to access the object's script just as you did when creating it.

Using Variables

The message handlers, commands, functions, and their arguments entered directly in the script are constant. Every time the script is executed, the same information is used, resulting in the same use of the command. In addition, HyperTalk includes several constants (see Chapter 5), many of which make the entry of special characters such the carriage return or line feed possible without having to refer to their ASCII codes.

Many times, entering the information to be processed directly into the script is inefficient because it limits the usefulness of the script to just one operation. Limiting the script to one operation is fine if you know ahead of time exactly what data will be used or when the script must always perform the same action; for example, using the Date function to enter the current date into a field of a card that is always to show today's date.

However, you will often encounter situations where you do not know ahead of time exactly what information a particular command or function is to use. A simple example of this is a stack where you set up fields into which you enter all your travel-related expenses for a particular business trip in each card. Undoubtedly, you will want the card to have a field that totals all of the travel expenses that you enter in the other fields. You will not know what the expense figures will be for any given business trip. Even if you did, creating a script to have HyperCard add those expenses would be of no use when you add a new card to track the expenses for the next business trip. The expenses that the script for the total field must add vary each time the commands in that script are executed.

To take care of these kinds of situations, you put the information into *variables*, which are temporary storage containers that hold the information for processing in the memory of the computer (RAM). Because variables reside solely in the memory of the computer, they are deleted when the commands in a script are finished being executed, when you go to a new stack, or when you quit HyperCard.

Variables are used in the following ways:

- To temporarily store information that is ultimately to be put into fields

- To store intermediate values to be calculated

- To store user input so that it can be validated before the variables are entered in fields

- To determine what action the script is to take according to what is entered into the variables

To create a variable in HyperTalk, you initialize it by assigning it a name at the same time you give it a starting value. This is done with the Put command (see Chapter 2). For example, to store the word *Yes* in a variable named *response*, you enter

put "Yes" into response

in the script. You can verify the contents (and existence) of any variable that you use by typing its name in the Message box. If the variable has not been defined or is no longer in use, HyperCard will return the message

Can't understand <variable name>

where *<variable name>* is the actual name you have entered into the Message box.

The program allows you to assign a variable any name so long as it is a single word. Remember that many words are already used by HyperTalk as part of its vocabulary. Although HyperTalk will allow you to use terms in its vocabulary as names for your variables, this is not a good idea because HyperCard will waste time trying to interpret the variable as a command or message. In addition, it can cause you a great deal of confusion when trying to understand the variable's function in the script.

Local versus Global Variables

When you create a variable, its contents are forgotten as soon as the message handler is finished executing the commands within it. This kind of variable is referred to as a *local variable*. Neither the name nor the contents of a local variable are remembered after the end of the message handler that uses it.

You can change a local variable into a global variable. The name and contents of global variables are remembered after the end of the handler that uses it. This means that their contents can be used in different scripts, even if those scripts are located in different stacks. The program remembers the name and contents of a global variable until you start a new application program from HyperCard or quit HyperCard.

All variables that you create in the scripts are local variables unless you declare them to be global variables with the Global command. To make a variable global, you simply list its name after the Global command (referred to as declaring the variable to be global). For example, you can make the *response* variable a global variable when you create it by entering

global response
put "Yes" into response

You can declare any number of variables to be global variables by separating their names with commas after the Global command, as in

global subtotal, ytd, grandtotal

Any variables that you define in the Message box are automatically global variables.

It is important to note that each time you reuse a global variable, be it in the card, background, field, or button script of the current or a different stack, you must also use the Global command to redeclare it as a global variable. It is not sufficient just to declare it to be a global variable once prior to initializing it in a particular script.

The It Variable

In HyperTalk, there are a few commands that make use of a special variable created by the program. This is the local variable named *it*. These commands include Get, Answer, Write, and Ask (see Chapter 2). In all cases, the information that the program gets either from the system, the HyperCard stacks, or the user in response to the use of one of these commands is placed in the variable *it*. Because Hyper-Talk uses this same variable for all four commands, its contents will change as these commands are executed.

If you use the *it* variable in the scripts that you write, be careful that HyperTalk does not overwrite its contents before your handler is finished using this information. Most of the time, it is easier and safer to have your script put the contents of the *it* variable into a new variable not used by any of the HyperTalk commands themselves.

The Selection Variable

In addition to the *it* variable that HyperTalk maintains and uses, the program also maintains a special variable named *selection*. Whenever you select text in a field by clicking and dragging over it, this text is placed in the *selection* variable.

The On CopyDown...End CopyDown message handler example (see Figure 1.2, earlier in this chapter) uses this variable to copy all selected text from a field into a new card in the References stack. You can create scripts like this that evaluate the contents of the *selection* variable and perform particular operations based on its contents.

HyperCard Containers

This is a good time to look more closely at the kinds of information containers used by HyperCard and the ways you can refer to individual pieces of information they can contain in the scripts that you write. Variables are only one type of container that hold information for processing in the program. Text fields, either in the background or card layer of a stack, are also containers of information. The Message box is yet another information container.

All information stored within these different containers is stored as text. Even when you enter only numbers into the Message box or a field, they are stored as text items. This simplifies matters a great deal because the program treats the contents of all containers alike. Even when the program calculates a new result with one of the math functions or HyperCard commands that perform arithmetic calculations, it does it by transforming any text that it deems should contain a value into a number to perform the calculation, and then storing the result of the calculation as text in the appropriate container.

The use of quotation marks to delimit text strings is often optional in scripts but, nevertheless, highly recommended. Text strings in HyperTalk text are best delimited by quotation marks; this ensures that HyperCard will not misinterpret the text as one of its commands or functions, or as a system message. For example, if you are referring to a card named Quit, you should enter

go to card "Quit"

If you don't enclose Quit in quotation marks, HyperCard will confuse the reference to the card named Quit with the system message Quit.

Values

Although values represent constants that are stored as text strings, they do not require quotation marks to avoid ambiguity. This is because values expressed as numbers do not contain any internal spaces (spaces are the natural delimiters of numbers). When entering values into a HyperTalk script, you can enter numbers up to ten by using their name rather than their symbol (that is, *ten* rather than *10*). For instance, you could enter

put ten + six into newNumber

or

put 10 + 6 into newNumber

In either case, the local variable *newNumber* will contain the sum of 16.

Text Components

When you use the text stored in these containers in a HyperTalk script, you can isolate specific text items by referring to them alone. This is especially helpful in the case of fields, which often contain many individual pieces of text information.

HyperTalk breaks the text stored in its containers into several distinct components:

Characters	Keyboard characters except for the space or comma
Words	Characters delimited by spaces
Items	Characters delimited by commas
Lines	Words and items delimited by carriage returns

Chunking Expressions

When you want to extract a particular piece of text, you can do so by referring to its text component by name and by the position it has in the container. This is referred to as a *chunking expression,* because it returns just a part (chunk) of the string requested. For example, assume you had the following text stored on the first line of the first field in the card:

Sandy, Jeff, Andy, and Keri Shewmaker

If you enter the chunking expression

put item 2 of field 1

the Message box will contain *Jeff* as the second item. To Hyper-Card, an *item* is any piece of text entered between commas. However, when HyperCard extracts an item, it does not include the comma as part of it.

If you enter

put word 2 of field 1

the contents of the Message box will be *Jeff,* (including the comma after his name). To HyperCard, *words* are any text separated by spaces. When it extracts a word, it includes any punctuation that is not separated by spaces.

You can have HyperCard extract just a single character of text from within a container. For example, if you enter

put char 1 of word 5 of field 1

the Message box will contain the *K* from Keri when you press the Return key.

When the field has multiple lines of text, you need to include the line number when setting up a chunking expression to extract specific text from it. For instance, if the fourth word of the second line of the third field in a card is *Suite*, you could copy it into the Message box by entering

put word 4 of line 2 of field 3

You can refer to the position of any element that you want to extract by the words *last*, *middle*, or the ordinal numbers *first* through *tenth*. You can also have the program extract a random piece of information by using the word *any* (as in *put any word of first field*). For instance, you could also enter the previous example to extract the word *Suite* by entering

put fourth word of second line of third field

Be careful not to use the definite article *the* before the first ten ordinal numbers, last, or middle. In other words, you cannot enter the statement

put the fourth word of the first field

It must be entered as

put fourth word of first field

to be accepted in a HyperCard command or function.

When you use the designation *middle*, you can abbreviate it to *mid*. Instead of entering the chunking expression

put second char of middle word of last line of third field

you can enter it as

put second char of mid word of last line of third field

Joining Text Components

Not only can you extract specific text components, but you can also join them. The technical name for this procedure of joining individual text items is *concatenation*. To have HyperCard concatenate two pieces of text, you use the **&** (ampersand). If you want the program to include a space between the items you join, you enter **&&** (double ampersand).

You can concatenate any text components. Assume that you had a person's first name entered into field 1 of a card and her last name entered into field 2. You could have both the first and last names put into the last field of the card by entering

put word 1 of field 1 && word 1 of field 2 into field 3

If *Susan* were entered into the first field and *Kelly* were entered in the second field, the third field would then contain

Susan Kelly

If you concatenate using only one ampersand (&), there will be no spaces between the text—they will be literally joined. In the example cited, using one ampersand would result in having

SusanKelly

entered into the third field. If you want more than one space between the text items you join, enter the required number of spaces enclosed in double quotation marks in-between the double ampersand, as in

&" "&

to have three spaces between the text items.

Because you have the power to extract specific text items and join them as you wish, you can control exactly what information is placed into or removed from any of the HyperCard information containers.

HyperTalk Control Structures

When a HyperTalk message handler finds a matching system message has been sent, it performs all of the commands found in that handler. Normally, these commands are carried out sequentially until the program executes an End statement that signals the end of the message handler. There are times, however, when you need to have HyperCard modify the order in which these commands are executed. HyperTalk provides five control structures for modifying this order: If, Repeat, Exit, Pass, and Send. Pass and Send are proper HyperTalk commands, and you will find information about them in Chapter 2. The If, Repeat, and Exit constructions are discussed at length in the following sections.

Creating Comparative Expressions

When a decision is to be made depending upon whether a particular condition or set of conditions is true or false in HyperCard, you need to set up a *true or false expression* as part of the If...Then construction. This true or false expression contains operative words that tell the program what is compared to what. There are several operative words and symbols that can be used in HyperTalk true or false expressions. These words and symbols are summarized in Table 1.2. They are referred to as Boolean operators after the nineteenth-century English mathematician, George Boole, who formulated the system of algebraic logic that requires their use.

Notice from this table that you can use either the English word *is* or the equal sign when setting up a true or false expression that tests the equality (sameness) of two elements. The other comparatives—such as greater than, less than, and the like—require the use of the mathematical symbols. When you need to use the *not equal to* operator, you press the $<$ (left angle bracket) followed by the $>$ (right angle bracket). Spaces between any of the compound symbols ($<>$, $>=$, and $<=$) are allowed.

When you need to express compound conditions as part of the true or false expression, you use the operators And or Or to join the expressions. When you use the And operator, both expressions must be true before HyperCard will take the action you assign to the

Operator	Meaning	Examples
= *or* is	Is equal to or is the same as	If field 1 is empty If field 6 = "CA"
>	Is greater than	If item 4 of the long date > 1988
<	Is less than	If the number of cards < 100
>= *or* > =	Is greater than or equal to	If the length of field 1 > = 35
<= *or* < =	Is less than or equal to	If chars in field 8 < = 1
<> *or* < >	Is unequal to or is not the same as	If field "Phone" < > empty If the number of card buttons < > 2
And	Both conditions must be true	If field 6 = "CA" and field 8 > 25 If it > = 200 and it < = 300

Or	One or the other condition must be true	If field 6 = empty or
		  field 6 = "NY"
		If field 2 > = 20 or
		  field 3 < = 85432

Not	Test for opposite condition	If field 6 is not "CA" If item 4 of the long date is not 1986

Table 1.2: The Boolean Operators in HyperTalk

true outcome. When you use the Or operator, only one of the expressions must test true for the program to take the action you assign to the true outcome. The Not operator works a lot like the < > operator except that it is used with one comparison and changes the result to its opposite. It is often combined with And and Or to create complex expressions.

From the examples in Table 1.2, you can see that you can test the content of the various components that are stored in a HyperCard container. This includes any variables that you create as well as the *it* and *selection* variables created and used by HyperTalk itself.

The If...Then Construction

In HyperTalk, the simplest If condition uses the If...Then construction as follows:

if <expression> then <command>

You can also phrase the same command somewhat differently:

If <expression>
then <command>

In the first case, the HyperCard command to be executed if the true or false expression is found to be true is placed on the same line. In the second example, the command and the operative word Then are placed on a line of their own directly beneath the If command and the true or false expression. How you want to enter an If...Then construction is completely up to you. If the true or false expression is somewhat lengthy (as is the case with some compound conditions), you may find it better to have the Then clause with the HyperTalk command on its own line.

For example, you can enter a condition to add a new card to the current stack if the *it* variable contains the word *yes* either as

if it = "yes" then doMenu "New Card"

or

if it = "yes"
then doMenu "New Card"

The If...Then constructions you create can have multiple commands that are to be carried out if the true or false expression is found to be true. When you designate multiple commands, you must alter the If...Then form somewhat and add an End If statement to the script, as follows:

if <expression> then
  <command>
  <command>
end if

For example, if you want multiple HyperCard commands to be carried out when the *it* variable contains the word *yes*, you would enter the If...Then construction in the following way:

```
if it = "yes" then
   doMenu "New Card"
   put the number of cards into the message box
   put the long date into field 5
end if
```

The End If statement tells HyperCard which commands belong to the If...Then construction and which do not. When you want the program to perform multiple commands if a particular condition (or conditions) is found to be true, you must remember to add the End If statement on its own line of the script.

The If...Then...Else Construction

When you want HyperCard to perform one command when the true or false expression is true and another command when it is false, you use the If...Then...Else construction. The Else operative word separates the command or commands that you want performed when the condition is found to be false from the command or commands that you want performed when the condition is true.

When there is only one command to be performed when the condition is true and one command to be performed when it is false, you can use either of the following forms:

```
if <expression> then <command> else <command>
```

(all on one line) or

```
if <expression> then <command> ¬
else <command>
```

For instance, if you wanted a new card added when the *it* variable contains *yes* and you wanted the program to return to the Home card when it contains anything else (or is empty), you could enter

```
if it = "yes" then doMenu "New Card" else go home
```

or

```
if it = "yes" then doMenu "New Card"
else go home
```

Again, you will have to decide which format you find easier to read. If the condition is long, then you will want to use the second form.

When using the If...Then...Else construction, you may find situations where you have multiple HyperTalk commands to be performed when the condition is true and only a single command to be performed when the condition is false. In such cases, you use the form

```
if <expression> then
  <command>
  <command>
else <command>
end if
```

Expanding on the previous example somewhat, you would enter the following:

```
if it = "yes" then
  doMenu "New Card"
  put the number of cards into the message box
else go home
end if
```

Notice that the two commands to be performed when *it* does contain yes are indented to set them off from the single Else command that is performed when *it* contains something else.

If the If...Then...Else construction has only a single command to be performed when the condition is true and multiple commands to be performed when the condition is false, you alter the format and terminate the construction with an End If statement. This has the following form:

```
if <expression> then <command>
else
  <command>
  <command>
end if
```

As an example, you could have this script:

```
if it = "yes" then doMenu "New Card"
else
   set userLevel to 1
   go first card
   show cards
end if
```

Notice in this example that indenting the commands beneath Else (those that are performed when *it* does not contain yes) set them off, thereby enhancing the overall legibility of the script.

You will also find times when your script must contain multiple HyperTalk commands that are to be performed both when the condition is true and when it is false. Under these circumstances, you need to include an End If statement and put the If...Then...Else construction into this form:

```
if <expression> then
   <command>
   <command>
else
   <command>
   <command>
end if
```

For example, you could use the following If...Then...Else construction:

```
If it = "yes" then
   doMenu "New Card"
   put the number of cards into the message box
else
   set userLevel to 1
   go first card
   show cards
end if
```

Nesting If...Then Constructions

You can put an If...Then construction within another If...Then construction in a script. This technique is referred to as *nesting*. When you nest If...Then constructions, the program helps you keep things straight by indenting each new If...Then construction to the next tab stop. By keeping the level of indentation the same for each If...Then construction, you can easily spot if a particular If...Then construction is missing an End If statement.

The script in Figure 1.3 contains one If...Then...Else construction nested within another. When the MouseUp message is detected by this handler, the program puts the system time into the *it* variable. There are three outcomes to be tested for in this message handler: the time is before noon, after noon, or 12:00 noon exactly. The first If clause returns the greeting "Good morning" if the time is found to be prior to (less than) 12:00 noon.

```
on mouseUp
     get the time
         if it < "12:00 PM" then
             put "Good morning" into the message box
         else
             if it > "12:00 PM" then
             put "Good afternoon" into the message box
             else
                 beep 12
                 put "Lunch time!" into the message box
             end if
         end if
end mouseUp
```

Figure 1.3: Nested If...Then...Else constructions

If this is not the case, then there are still two possible outcomes: it is noon or it is some time after noon. To test for this, a second If...Then...Else construction is introduced. The If clause of this construction returns the "Good afternoon" greeting if the time is after (greater than) 12:00 noon. If this is not true, then it must be 12:00 noon precisely, so the Macintosh sounds 12 beeps and informs you that it's time for lunch.

Notice the formatting involved with the nested If...Then...Else constructions. The If, Else, and End If clauses for the first (outer) If...Then...Else construction are all indented to the same level. Likewise, these clauses for the second (inner) If...Then...Else construction are all indented to the same level, one more tab stop in. When nesting If...Then...Else constructions, you must terminate each construction with an End If statement. Note, too, that all of these conditional statements are indented in one tab from the On MouseUp...End MouseUp message handler statements, which are aligned with each other (flush left in the Script Editor).

The Repeat Constructions

In addition to allowing you control the operations performed by a particular script conditionally, as with the If...Then construction, HyperTalk allows you to control the number of times a particular command or set of commands is repeated. It does this through the use of four different Repeat constructions, using the commands Repeat For, Repeat While, Repeat Until, and Repeat With. The commands that you want repeated by the particular Repeat construction are referred to as a *loop*. The purpose of the Repeat construction is to repeat loops until a particular number of repetitions have been made or a particular condition is met or ceases to exist.

Although each of these Repeat constructions requires slightly different arguments, they do share a common form:

- The particular Repeat command and its arguments, which instruct the program how many times to repeat a loop, are entered on a single line of the script.

- The commands in the loop (that is, the commands to be repeated) are entered indented and are entered on the lines below the Repeat command (each command on its own line).

- The loop is terminated with an End Repeat statement entered on a line of its own immediately below the last command in the loop. This statement is automatically outdented so that it is aligned with the Repeat command.

The format of the Repeat constructions is important. By placing the commands in the loop between the Repeat command and the End Repeat command, HyperCard knows exactly what commands are to be repeated and in what order.

In the simplest form, the Repeat construction instructs HyperCard to perform the loop a set number of times. In its more complex forms, it instructs the program to continue to repeat the loop until a particular condition is met or while a particular condition is still true. When you use the Repeat construction in this way, you are actually having the program perform a type of decision-making somewhat akin to that performed with the If...Then construction.

The Repeat For Construction

The Repeat For construction simply tells HyperCard to repeat the command or commands in the loop for a particular number of times. Its form is as follows:

```
repeat [for] <number> [times]
   <command>
   <command>
end repeat
```

As you can see, the use of the command words *for* and *times* are optional. In other words, you can enter

```
repeat 10
```

or

```
repeat for 10
```

or even

```
repeat for 10 times
```

with the same result. In each case, the commands entered on subsequent lines of the Script Editor before the required End Repeat statement are executed ten times in the order in which they are listed.

For example, you could create a button that would add five cards to the current stack when it is used with the following script:

```
on mouseUp
   repeat for 5 times
      doMenu "New Card"
   end repeat
end mouseUp
```

When the MouseUp message is detected by the On MouseUp...End MouseUp message handler, the Repeat construction is executed. It instructs HyperCard to perform the *doMenu "New Card"* command five times, thus adding five new cards to the stack.

When specifying the <*number*> argument, you do not have to enter a particular value. This argument can be supplied as a result of a calculation (provided the calculation results in a whole number), as in the following:

```
on mouseUp
  repeat for round(the number of cards/4) times
    doMenu "New Card"
  end repeat
end mouseUp
```

In this case, the $<number>$ argument is not a constant number: if the stack contains 20 cards, the loop is repeated five times (20/4 = 5); if the stack contains eight cards, it is repeated only two times (8/4 = 2), and so on. The addition of the Round function, which rounds a fractional number up to the nearest whole number, prevents the $<number>$ argument from being anything but a whole number.

The $<number>$ argument can also be supplied from a HyperCard container such as the *it* variable or a field, provided that the container holds a whole number. You can make the new card button much more open-ended by modifying the button script to the following:

```
on mouseUp
  ask "How many cards do you want to add?" with 1
  repeat it
    doMenu "New Card"
  end repeat
end mouseUp
```

In this case, the Repeat construction uses the number you enter in the dialog box that appears as a result of the Ask command. This number is stored in the *it* variable, which is used as the $<number>$ argument of the Repeat For command.

The Repeat While and Repeat Until Constructions

The Repeat While and Repeat Until constructions both require a true or false expression as their arguments. In this way, they are just like the If...Then and If...Then...Else constructions. The form of the Repeat While construction is as follows:

```
repeat while <expression>
   <command>
   <command>
end repeat
```

In this case, the commands in the loop are repeated while the true or false expression remains true. As soon as the expression is found to be false, the loop is no longer repeated.

The form of the Repeat Until construction is similar:

```
repeat until <expression>
   <command>
   <command>
end repeat
```

However, it works just the opposite of the Repeat While construction. The commands in its loop are repeated only *until* the true or false expression is found to be true. In other words, the loop is repeated while the expression remains false.

For example, you could create a button script that takes you to the first address card in the current stack whose State field contains the state you specify in an Ask dialog box:

```
on mouseUp
   ask "Enter state code of the card you want to see:"
   if it is not empty then
      repeat while field "State" <> it
         go to next card
      end repeat
   end if
end mouseUp
```

However, you can create the same button script using the Repeat Until construction, as follows:

```
on mouseUp
   ask "Enter state code of the card you want to see:"
   if it is not empty then
      repeat until field "State" = it
```

```
        go to next card
      end repeat
    end if
  end mouseUp
```

Thus, when you use the Repeat While construction, the expression is phrased in the negative:

repeat while field "State" < > it

When you use the Repeat Until construction, the expression is phrased in the positive:

repeat until field "State" = it

With the Repeat While construction, the *go to next card* command is repeated while the state code in the State field is not the same as the reply that is stored in the *it* variable. As soon as the state code in the card is equal to the contents of the *it* variable, the loop is no longer repeated. With the Repeat Until construction, the Go command is repeated until the state code in the State field is the same as the reply stored in the *it* variable. As soon as this is true, its loop is no longer repeated.

Beware of endless loops in your scripts! For example, if you enter a state code in the Ask dialog box that does not match any of the state abbreviations entered in the State field of the cards in the stack, HyperCard will repeat the *go to next card* command endlessly. The only way to stop endless loops is by pressing the Command-period key combination.

The Repeat With Construction

In the Repeat With construction, you initialize a counter variable with a start number and give a stop number, thereby establishing the number of times the loop will be repeated. Each time HyperCard repeats the loop, it increases (or decreases) the counter by one until the counter equals the stop number. When you want the program to increase the counter by one each time a loop is executed, you use this form of the command:

**repeat with <variable> = <start number> to ¬
<stop number>**

```
  <command>
  <oommand>
end repeat
```

When you want the program to decrease the counter by one each time a loop is executed, you use this form of the command:

```
repeat with <variable> = <start number> down ¬
to <stop number>
  <command>
  <command>
end repeat
```

When you increment the counter (using the first form), the start number must be smaller than the stop number. This is just like counting up from one number to another by ones. When you decrement the counter (using the second form), just the opposite is true: the start number must be larger than the stop number. This is just like counting down from one number to another by ones.

As is true with the <*number*> argument in the Repeat For command, the <*start number*> and <*stop number*> arguments can be numbers that you enter directly into the script, or they can be supplied by calculations or HyperCard containers that return whole numbers. For example, you can enter the following:

```
on mouseUp
  repeat with counter = 1 to 10
    print this card
    go to next card
  end repeat
end mouseUp
```

In this case, the start and stop numbers for the counter are entered values. When the MouseUp message is sent, the print loop will always be repeated ten times, printing the next ten cards. However, you could also have the start and/or stop number supplied from a HyperCard container such as the *it* variable, as in the following script:

```
on mouseUp
  ask "How many cards to print?" with 1
  if it is not empty then
```

```
      repeat with counter = 1 to it
        print this card
        go to next card
      end repeat
    end if
  end mouseUp
```

Here, the number of times the print loop is repeated depends upon the number you enter in the dialog box in response to the Ask command.

The Repeat With command provides you with a useful algorithm that ensures a particular operation specified in the repeated loop will be applied to all the cards in the stack. This algorithm is

repeat with counter = 1 to the number of cards

By setting the start number at 1 and the stop number equal to the total number of cards, the loop to be repeated will always be applied to all the cards in the stack.

The Next Repeat Command

Normally, you want all of the commands entered into a loop that is to be repeated to be executed. However, there may be times when you only want all of the commands in a loop executed when a particular condition exists. In such cases, you can use the Next Repeat command to tell HyperCard which commands are to be skipped when a particular condition exists.

The Next Repeat command is used with the If...Then construction. The program uses this construction to evaluate a true or false expression, and the Next Repeat command is entered as the <*command*> argument after the Then conjunction. Only when the expression is false will the program execute the commands in the loop that follows the If...Then construction. If the expression is true, the Next Repeat command instructs HyperCard to return to the top of the Repeat construction. If you are using the Repeat For or Repeat With construction, the counter is incremented by one at this time.

The Repeat Next command can be used with any Repeat construction. The general format of the construction is shown here with the Repeat With construction:

```
repeat with <variable> = <start number> to ¬
<stop number>
    <command>
    <command>
    if <expression> then next repeat
        <command>
end repeat
```

For instance, assume that you have already sorted an address stack and copied all the cards where the state is New York to a separate address stack. Now you want to delete all the cards in the stack where the state (the State field) is New York (they are all redundant). To do that, you create a conditional delete button with this script:

```
on mouseUp
    ask "Enter the state code to delete for:"
    if it is not empty then
        repeat with counter = 1 to the number of cards
            go to next card
            if field "State" <> it then next repeat
                doMenu "Delete Card"
        end repeat
    end if
end mouseUp
```

When the MouseUp message is detected by the handler, the Ask command prompts you to enter the two-letter state code. In this particular example, you would enter NY into the dialog box to have all of the cards where the state code is NY deleted from the stack.

The Ask command stores this response in the *it* variable. Because the first If...Then expression is true (it is not empty), the Repeat With construction is executed. It contains the algorithm (*counter = 1 to the number of cards*) to have all the cards in the stack used. Therefore, the first command in this loop, *go to next card*, is executed for every card in the stack.

However, the second command, *doMenu "Delete Card"*, is executed conditionally. Only when the contents of the State field in the card are the same as NY (stored in the *it* variable) is this command carried out. This is because when the state code is not the same as NY, the <*expression*> argument of the second If...Then construction is true. When this is the case, the Next Repeat command is carried out. This command returns control to the top of the loop and increases the counter by one, thereby bypassing the *doMenu "Delete Card"* command on the line below it.

This entire procedure is then repeated until the number stored in the counter variable is equal to the total number of cards. As the result, all the cards where the state is NY will be deleted from the stack.

The Exit Command

When you are working with HyperCard's control structures, there may be times when you want to have the program escape the control of the structure prematurely when a particular condition is met. To meet such a need, you can use one of the forms of the HyperTalk Exit command. If you are exiting from an If...Then or If...Then...Else construction, you use the Exit If form of the command. If you are exiting from a Repeat construction, you use the Exit Repeat form of the command. If you are exiting from a message handler, you use the form

exit <message>

where the <*message*> argument is the name of the message in the handler. For example, if you were using an Exit command to prematurely leave an On MouseUp...End MouseUp message handler, you would enter the Exit command as

exit mouseUp

in the script.

The Exit commands are normally used with an If...Then construction of their own. This expression evaluates when the condition exists under which the control of the message handler, If...Then construction, or Repeat construction is to be terminated. Commonly, you will need to use the Exit command with a form of the Repeat construction, as in the following script:

on mouseUp
  ask "How many cards do you want to add?"

```
if it is not empty then
   repeat with counter = 1 to It
      if counter > 100 then exit repeat
         doMenu "New Card"
   end repeat
end if
End mouseUp
```

As used in this example, the Exit Repeat command limits the maximum number of cards that can be added with this button script to 100.

For example, if the user specifies a number of cards larger than 100 should be added, the loop with the *doMenu "New Card"* command will be faithfully executed only until the number of repetitions stored in the counter variable reaches 101 (exceeding 100 by one). At that time, the If...Then expression will become true, and the Exit Repeat command will be executed. This causes the program to stop processing the Repeat construction (so that no more cards will be added to the stack) and to begin executing the commands beyond the End Repeat statement. In this case, these commands include the End If and End MouseUp statements.

However, when the user specifies any number less than or equal to 100 in the Ask dialog box, the Exit Repeat command will not be executed before the stop number stored in the counter variable in the Repeat With construction is reached.

In a similar manner, when you use the Exit If command, the Exit command causes the program to break out of the If...Then or If...Then...Else construction when the true or false expression in its own If...Then construction becomes true. If you are using the Exit command with the *<message>* argument, it causes the program to break out of the message handler entirely when this is the case.

Calculations in Scripts

HyperCard can perform mathematical operations using either arithmetic operators or the HyperTalk arithmetic commands (see Chapter 2) or math functions (see Chapter 3). You can enter these operators, commands, and functions as part of scripts that you write, or you can enter them directly into the Message box. When you enter a calculation directly into the Message box, you are using it like an on-line calculator to obtain results that may, or may not, have anything to do with the contents of the current stack.

When you have the program perform math operations in the scripts you write, you can have the results stored in fields. You can also use variables to store intermediate results that are ultimately stored in fields of the cards in the current stack or other stacks. Although the results of math calculations are stored as text with whatever precision is returned by the calculations, you can modify the precision (the number of decimal places), the value, or the format by the use of various HyperTalk functions (see the Round and Trunc functions in Chapter 3 and the NumberFormat property in Chapter 4).

Included as part of the math operations are those that deal with dates and times (see the Date and Time functions in Chapter 3). HyperCard allows you to store dates and times in a variety of formats. It also allows you to peform arithmetic calculations between dates or times stored in various text fields.

Using the Arithmetic Operators

The arithmetic operators are **+** for addition, **−** for subtraction, ***** for multiplication, and **/** for division. In addition, you can raise one number by the power of a second number by using the **^** operator and control the way any remainders in division are handled with the operators *div* and *mod*. Any of these operators can be used with values or containers that hold values entered directly in the Message box to calculate results. For example, you can enter

30 * 5

which would give you the result of 150, or

field 2 * .5

which would give you half of the value stored in field 2 of the current card. This assumes, of course, that field 2 contains a value or an expression that returns a bona fide value. If it did not, HyperCard would display an Error Message dialog box informing you that it did not understand the use of *field*.

When you use the arithmetic operators to perform calculations in the scripts you write, you need to store the results either in a variable or in some other HyperCard container, such as another field or the Message box itself. You would never just enter an expression such as 50 * 3 on a line of a script, for the program would not know where to store the result. You must specify some container that will hold the new value. Quite often, this container will be a new field in the card.

In stacks that deal with numbers—sales, inventory items, and the like—you can set up calculated fields whose contents are supplied from an arithmetic operation peformed between other fields in the card. For example, if you have a stack that inventories the items that you sell on each card, you could have calculated fields in each card that show the dollar amount tied up in stock as well as the margin of profit. The contents of these calculated fields would be determined by the values entered in the stock, cost, and price fields in the card.

The calculations would all take place as the result of arithmetic operations between fields defined by the arithmetic operators. If field 3 contains the number of items in stock and field 4 the cost per item, you could have HyperCard store the dollar amount in stock in field 7 by entering

put field 3 * field 4 into field 7

in the background or stack script. Likewise, you could add a similar Put command in the script to determine the profit margin for each item and store it in the appropriate field.

Controlling Remainders in Division

When performing the arithmetic operation of division, you normally use the slash (/) as the operator—as in 9/2, which would result in 4.5. However, HyperCard gives you two additional operators for division, each of which controls any remainder that results from the division in a slightly different way. If you want any remainder to be discarded, you use *div* as the operator, as in

9 div 2

In this case, the program returns the answer of 4 because it drops the remainder of 1 and therefore does not include ½ or 0.5 in the answer.

If you want only the remainder to be used, you use *mod* as the operator. For example, entering

9 mod 2

produces 1 as the answer, because 1 is left over after 2 goes into 9 four times.

You can use the mod operator to determine if a number is odd or even. All odd numbers have a remainder of 1 when divided by 2, and all even numbers do not have any remainder (two goes into the number evenly). For example, to test if a number is even, you can enter something like this:

if testNumber mod 2 is 0 then ...

The If...Then construction is true only when the value entered into the *testNumber* variable is even, and therefore results in a zero remainder when divided with the mod operator.

Operators and Their Precedence

Table 1.3 shows you the order of operator precedence normally followed by the program when evaluating any kind of mathematical expression.

Any operator occurring in an expression that is on a higher level of this table is evaluated before those on a lower level of the table, regardless of the order in which they occur in that expression. Any operator on the same level in the table is equal in precedence and, in such a case, is evaluated in a strict left-to-right order. For example, when the operators for addition and subtraction occur in the same expression, the addition is performed before the subtraction only if its operator occurs first in the expression (when going from left to right).

As you can see from Table 1.3, you can alter the order of operator precedence with the use of parentheses, which are always evaluated first. When several levels of nested parentheses are added to an expression, they are always evaluated from inside out. For example, in the expression

10*2 ^ 2 + 3

the ^ (exponent) operator is evaluated first, so that 2 is squared

Order	Operators	Operation
1	Operators within parentheses are evaluated before those outside of parentheses	
2	− (signifying negative value), Not	
3	^	Raising a number by a power
4	*, /, div, mod	Multiplication and division
5	+, −	Addition and subtraction
6	&, &&	Concatenation
7	>, <, > =, < =, contains, is in	
8	=, < >	
9	And	
10	Or	

Table 1.3: The Order of Precedence Followed by HyperCard

resulting in 4. Next, the * (multiplication) operator is evaluated, so that 10 is multiplied by 4 resulting in 40. Finally, the + (addition) operator is evaluated, so that 3 is added to 40 giving an answer of 43.

If the same expression is rephrased with the use of parentheses, you get quite a different result:

```
10*(2 ^ 2 + 3)
```

This time, the expression within the parentheses is evaluated first, so that the 2 is squared and then is added to 3 resulting in 7. Then, this result is multiplied by 10 giving you the answer of 70.

When HyperTalk math functions are mixed in an expression with other arithmetic operations, they are always calculated first. In other words, they act like parentheses in altering the order of calculation in their favor. For example, in the expression

```
sqrt(49)*5 + 2
```

the Sqrt function is evaluated first and returns 7 as the result. Then, 7 is multiplied by 5 and the product of 35 is added to 2, returning the answer of 37. However, you can still alter the order in which the multiplication and addition take place in this expression with the use of parentheses:

```
sqrt(49)*(5 + 2)
```

In this case, the square root of 49 returns 7, which is multiplied by the sum of 7 (5 + 2), giving you the answer of 49 instead of 37.

Building Your Own Functions

HyperCard enables you to create functions of your own in the scripts that you write. These functions can include those that perform mathematical calculations or those that peform other functions, such as returning part of the date or time. When you define your own function, you follow this form:

```
function <function name> [parameter]
    <command>
    <command>
    return <value>
end <function name>
```

When entering commands in the new function that calculate results, you use *return* as the operative word. Note that this use of *return* to have the program perform a designated calculation as part of a user-defined function is limited strictly to this usage. Normally, Hyper-Card interprets the return in a script as a constant that substitutes for pressing the Return key on the keyboard.

You can use the Function construction to define any often-used formulas as functions, which are easier to enter in your scripts. For example, to calculate the monthly payment due for a loan amortized at a set rate of interest, you can create a Payment function. In the card or background script of the stack, you would enter the following commands to define the Payment function:

```
function payment x, y, z
    return x*(y/(1 - (1 + y) ^ - z))
end payment
```

Then, you can apply the Payment function as you would any other HyperTalk function. For example, you could add it to a button script like this:

```
on mouseUp
  ask "Enter the amount of the loan:"
  put it into x
  ask "Enter yearly interest rate:"
  put it/12 into y
  ask "Enter term of the loan in years:"
  put it * 12 into z
  put payment(x,y,z) into field "Monthly Payment"
end mouseUp
```

You can also create functions that return just part of a date or time. For instance, you could create Year and Month functions that return just the year or month part of the date. For the Year function, you could enter the following commands to the stack or background script:

```
function year date
  get date
  convert it to dateItems
  return item 1 of it
end year
```

After defining it, you can use it in a button script like this:

```
on closeField
  put year(the date) into field 5
end closeField
```

To define the Month function that returns just the name of the month, you could enter these commands in the stack or background script:

```
function month date
  get date
  convert it to long date
  return word 1 of item 2 of it
end month
```

You can then use the newly defined Month function in the stack as you would use any other function in HyperCard.

CHAPTER **2**

The HyperTalk Commands

The commands of HyperTalk make up the largest part of the language's vocabulary. Moreover, the commands represent the most essential components of the message handlers entered into the scripts that you write. Each command has its own form (structure), comprised of a command word or words followed by its arguments, which specify what exactly it is to accomplish. If you are unfamiliar with the notation scheme used to show which command words and arguments are required, optional, can vary, or must remain constant, refer to the section on Programming Conventions Used in This Book in the Introduction. Although the HyperTalk commands are difficult to adequately categorize, they can be classified into several broad categories: browsing, arithmetic, screen manipulation, sound, file manipulation, and HyperCard object manipulation commands (see Table 2.1).

The HyperTalk commands in this chapter are arranged in alphabetical order from Add to Write. If you need more information on how HyperTalk commands are used in scripts or with the HyperTalk control structures, refer to Chapter 1. In the section on Extending the HyperTalk Message Vocabulary, you will find information on how you can create your own commands as message handlers that can be referred to by name.

ARITHMETIC COMMANDS

add <source> to <destination>

divide <destination> by <source>

multiply <destination> by <source>

subtract <source> from <destination>

BROWSING COMMANDS

find <source> [in <field n>]

find chars <source> [in <field n>]

find word <source> [in <field n>]

go [to] <destination>

help

show [<number> | all] cards

FILE MANIPULATION COMMANDS

close file <fileName>

close printing

open [<document> with] <application>

open file <document>

open printing [with dialog]

print [all | <number> cards | this card]

print <document> with <application>

read from file <fileName> until <character>

read from file <fileName> for <number of bytes>

write <source> to file <fileName>

Table 2.1: HyperTalk Commands by Category

HYPERCARD OBJECT MANIPULATION COMMANDS

choose <tool name> tool

convert <container> to <format>

delete <component>

dial <source> [with modem [<modemParameters>]]

do <source>

doMenu <name of menu item>

edit script of <object>

exit <message>

get <expression>

global <variable name>

pass <message>

pop card [into <container>]

push [this | recent] card

put <source> before | into | after <destination>

reset paint

send <message> to <target>

set <property> of <object> to <value>

sort [ascending | descending] [text | numeric | international | dateTime] by <field or expression>

type <source> [with shiftKey | optionKey | commandKey]

wait [for] <number of ticks>

wait [for] <number> seconds

wait until <true or false expression>

wait while <true or false expression>

Table 2.1: HyperTalk Commands by Category (continued)

SCREEN MANIPULATION COMMANDS

answer <question> [with <reply> [or <reply> [or <reply>]]]

ask <question> [with <default>]

click at <location> [with shiftKey | optionKey | commandKey]

drag from <h,v> to <h,v> [with shiftKey | optionKey | commandKey]

hide menubar | card window | <window> | <field or button>

show menubar | card window | <window> | <field or button> [at <location>]

visual [effect] <name of effect> [speed] [to black | white | gray]

SOUND COMMANDS

beep [<number>]

play <voice> [tempo <tempo number>] [<notes>]

Table 2.1: HyperTalk Commands by Category (continued)

Add

Adds the contents of the <*source*> to the <*destination*> and puts the answer in the container specified as the <*destination*> argument.

FORM

add <**source**> **to** <**destination**>

ARGUMENTS

<*source*>   Any value or expression that produces a value when evaluated. This value can be stored in any HyperCard container.

<*destination*>   Any HyperCard container, such as a field, a variable, or the Message box. The result is stored in the <*destination*> argument.

USAGE

The Add command allows you to perform the operation of addition in a script. The result of the addition is stored in the <*destination*> argument. This means that the value originally held in this container will be replaced by the calculated sum. To preserve the two values that are to be summed, use a variable as an intermediate storage container (see the second example that follows).

EXAMPLES

add 5 to field 1

If field 1 contains 10 prior to the execution of this Add command, it will contain 15 after execution.

```
on mouseUp
   add field "Item 1" to tempSum
   add field "Item 2" to tempSum
   put tempSum into field "Total"
end mouseUp
```

This example uses *tempSum* as an intermediate storage container.

NOTE

You can also perform the operation of addition in a script by using the + (plus) sign between two values or two HyperCard containers that hold values, as in

```
put field 1 + field 2 into field 5
```

SEE ALSO

Subtract command
Multiply command
Divide command

Answer

Prompts the user to choose up to three possible replies that are displayed in a dialog box along with the text of the prompt or question. The reply chosen is stored in the *it* variable.

FORM

answer <**question**> [**with** <**reply**> [**or** <**reply**>
[**or** <**reply**>]]]

ARGUMENTS

<*question*>   These arguments can consist of any text
and <*reply*>   string, but it must be enclosed in a pair of
                  quotation marks.

USAGE

The Answer command enables you to prompt the user to choose between alternate replies. The command displays your question in a typical Macintosh dialog box above the alternate replies. These replies appear within buttons using the round rectangle shape. The last <*reply*> argument is automatically highlighted, making it the default that can be selected by pressing the Return or Enter key as well as by clicking on its button. To select one of the other (nondefault) replies, the user must move the pointer to its button and click on it.

The text of the <*reply*> argument selected is stored in the *it* variable, where it can be tested with an If...Then construction to determine which steps the script is to carry out next. The Answer command is useful in educational and training applications, where it can be used to quiz the student and record correct and incorrect responses.

EXAMPLES

answer "Delete this card?" with "Yes" or "No"

answer "Go to which card?" with "First" or "Last" or "Home"

NOTE

HyperCard uses the Chicago font to display the <*question*> and <*reply*> arguments in the dialog box. You cannot change the font or text size. Make sure that your question is short enough to fit in the dialog box and that your replies will fit within the space allotted for the buttons. The exact number of characters that can be accommodated depends upon the width of the characters entered into the dialog box.

SEE ALSO

Ask command

Ask

Prompts the user to answer a question with a default reply or a reply of his or her own presented in a dialog box. The response chosen is stored in the *it* memory variable. If used in the *ask password* form, the reply entered by the user is stored as an encrypted number in the *it* variable.

FORMS

ask <**question**> [**with** <**default**>]

ask password <**question**>

ARGUMENTS

<*question*>   These arguments can consist of any text
and <*default*>   string, but it must be enclosed in a pair of
quotation marks.

USAGE

The Ask command has two uses: you can use it either to obtain information from the user that can be used to determine the next steps taken in the script, or to obtain a password, which can be stored in a field (as an encrypted number), that must be matched in order for the user to be able to use the stack.

The Ask command displays your question in a typical Macintosh dialog box above a line that contains the text of the default reply; if no <*default*> argument is specified, this line is blank. Beneath the reply line, the dialog box contains Cancel and OK buttons. To accept the default reply or a reply that has been entered by the user on the reply line, either click on the OK button or press the Return or Enter key (the OK button is highlighted). The user can edit the default reply or type over it (the default reply is selected for quick editing) before choosing the OK button.

The text string entered in response to the Ask command is stored in the *it* variable, where it can be tested with an If...Then construction to determine which steps the script is to carry out next. The Ask command is useful in any situation where you need to prompt the user for a response that determines what happens next in the script.

EXAMPLES

    ask "How many cards to print?" with 1

    ask "What is your name?" with userName

    ask password "Please enter your password."

NOTE

Like the Answer command, the Ask command uses the Chicago font (this cannot be changed). The reply that you enter for the <*default*> argument or that the user enters during the execution of the Ask command cannot exceed the length of the line in the dialog box. The exact number of characters that can be accommodated on this line depends upon the width of the characters entered into the dialog box. Generally, you can enter no more than 40 characters as a reply to the Ask command.

SEE ALSO

Answer command

Beep

Sounds the bell the number of times specified.

FORM

beep [<**number**>]

ARGUMENT

[<*number*>]   This argument must contain a value, an
expression that returns a value, or a container
that holds such a value or expression. If the
<*number*> argument is omitted, the Beep
command sounds the bell once.

USAGE

The Beep command is used to sound a warning bell. It is useful
when you want to alert the user to some change that has occurred or
is about to occur in the current card or stack.

EXAMPLES

beep 3

beep 2 * field 3

beep beepNumber

where *beepNumber* is a variable containing a value.

SEE ALSO

Play command

Choose

Selects a new tool from the Tools menu.

FORM

choose <**tool name**> **tool**

ARGUMENTS

The names of tools on the Tools menu that can be used as the <*tool name*> argument are as follows:

browse	spray
button	rectangle
field	round rect
select	bucket
lasso	oval
pencil	curve
brush	text
eraser	regular polygon
line	polygon

The word *tool* must be added to the <*tool name*> argument of the Choose command. The <*tool name*> argument can be a Hyper-Card container, such as a field or variable, that holds the name of the tool to be chosen.

USAGE

The Choose command allows you to select various tools from the Tools menu in a script just as though you had selected them from the menu with a mouse. This command is frequently used with the DoMenu command to enable the script to enact a particular HyperCard menu option. It can also be used when the script calls for adding graphics to a card. In such a case, it is used to select the appropriate drawing tool (pencil, line, rectangle, and so on) before using a Drag command.

When using the Choose command to select a tool other than the Browse tool, be sure to use it later on in the same message handler to once again select the Browse tool, if you want the user to be able to browse the stack or edit text fields. This is especially true in stacks where the Menu bar has been hidden (see the Hide command for information on how to do this).

| EXAMPLES |

choose browse tool

choose text tool

choose useTool

where *useTool* is the name of a local variable, which contains both the tool name and the word *tool*, as in *spray tool*.

| NOTE |

The user level must be set to either the Painting, Authoring, or Scripting level before the Choose command can be used.

| SEE ALSO |

DoMenu command
Drag command
UserLevel (global) property: Chapter 4

Click

Clicks the mouse at a specified location in the screen.

FORM

   click at <**location**> [**with shiftKey** | **optionKey**
   | **commandKey**]

ARGUMENTS

<*location*>   Specified by the horizontal and vertical
                      screen coordinates where you want the click-
                      ing to occur. The horizontal and vertical
                      coordinates must be separated by a comma.
                      The Macintosh screen coordinates are num-
                      bered from 0,0 at the upper left corner to
                      512,342 at the lower right corner. You can
                      also specify the <*location*> argument with a
                      function (such as *ClickLoc*) or a property
                      (such as *loc of field 3*) that returns such screen
                      coordinates, or with a container that holds
                      the number of the horizontal and vertical
                      coordinates.

with shiftKey,   Use these optional arguments to simulate
with   clicking at a particular location with these
optionKey,   keys depressed.
and *with com-*
mandKey

USAGE

The Click command simulates moving the mouse to a particular
position on the HyperCard screen and clicking the mouse button. It

is often used prior to the Type command when a script is to enter text starting at a particular position in a card. It can also be used to position the cursor when entering paint text from a script with the Text tool.

EXAMPLES

click at 26,160

click at 15,100 with commandKey

click at loc of field 2

click at mouseLoc with shiftKey

put mouseH into hPixel
put mouseV into vPixel
click at hPixel, vPixel

where *hPixel* and *vPixel* are local memory variables.

SEE ALSO

Type command
ClickLoc and MouseLoc functions: Chapter 3
Location (field and button) properties: Chapter 4

Close File

Closes the file after importing or exporting data to and from Hyper-Card and another application program.

FORM

   close file <**fileName**>

ARGUMENT

   <fileName>   Enter the name of the file that has been opened with the Open File command for the *<fileName>* argument. If the file name contains spaces, be sure to enclose the name in a pair of quotation marks. The *<fileName>* argument can also be supplied by a variable that already contains the name of the file that was opened.

USAGE

The Close File command is used to close the file once information has been imported or exported using the Read and Write commands. It must be preceded by an Open File command. The Close File statement ensures that the file is secure from any further data transfer (and possible corruption).

EXAMPLES

   close file "Client List"
   close file transferFile

where *transferFile* is a variable that contains the file name.

NOTE ═══════════════

The Close File command must come after the Open File command in the script and be part of the same message handler.

SEE ALSO ═══════════════

Open File command
Read command
Write command

Close Printing

See Open Printing

Convert

Converts the date or time entered into a HyperCard container to a specified format.

FORM

convert <**container**> **to** <**format**>

ARGUMENTS

<*container*>   The name of the container (field, variable, or the Message box) that holds the date or time.

<*format*>   The formats that can be specified for the <*format*> argument include the following:

Format	Explanation/Example
seconds	The seconds since 1904
long date	Friday, December 25, 1989
short date	12/25/89
abbreviated date	Fri, Dec 25, 1989
long time	3:15:20 PM
short time	3:15 PM
dateItems	Integers representing the year, month, and day in a date (as in 1989,12,25) or those representing the hour, minute, and seconds in the time (as in 03,15,20).

USAGE

The Convert command is used to convert a date or time that has been entered in a container such as a field or variable to a new format. You can use the Convert command to alter the display of the date or to format the time in a particular way.

The Convert command is often used when creating a script that performs arithmetic between dates. In such a case, the dates to be used are converted to the *seconds* format before the arithmetic is performed. The result in seconds is then divided by the appropriate factor (24*60*60 for days, 24*60*60*7 for weeks, and so on) to display the result in the desired units (see the last example in the following section).

The short date, abbreviated date, long date, short time, and long time formats are identical to those used by the Date and Time functions except that they are not preceded by *the*. The dateItems format lists each component of the date and time as an equivalent number. These items are, from left to right in the list, the year, the month, the day, the hour, the minutes, the seconds, and the day of the week (with Sunday equal to 1 and Saturday equal to 7). This can be used with the *item* text component to return just a part of the date or time that has been converted to the dateItems format (see the second example in the following section).

EXAMPLES

convert field 1 to abbreviated date

convert returnTime to dateItems
put item 1 of returnTime into field 4

places the year (*dateItem 1*) from the returnTime variable into field 4.

on closeField
 convert field "Depart" to seconds
 convert field "Return" to seconds
 put field "Return" into returnDate
 subtract field "Depart" from returnDate
 put returnDate/(24*60*60) into field "Trip Duration"

```
  convert field "Depart" to short date
  convert field "Return" to short date
end closeField
```

This script subtracts the date in the Depart field from that in the Return field (both converted to seconds from January 1, 1904). The result in days (obtained by dividing the seconds by 24*60*60 to get the number of days) is then placed in the Trip Duration field. Finally, the dates in the Depart and Return fields (now held in seconds) are converted back to the short date format.

SEE ALSO

Date and Time functions: Chapter 3

Delete

Deletes text in a specific component of a container such as a field or variable.

FORM

   delete <component>

ARGUMENT

   <component>   Refers to the text component or chunk expression of the string in a HyperCard container. These parts of strings or chunks can be as follows:

Container	Explanation
character or char	Individual character
item	All characters up to, but not including, a comma
word	All characters up to, but not including, a space
line	All characters up to, but not including, the carriage return

Chunks are specified from the smallest to the largest text component. Each chunk in the expression is separated by the word *of*, and the expression is terminated with the name of the HyperCard container. If necessary, you can include a reference to the card and/or stack if the container is a field that is not on the card currently displayed when the Delete command is executed.

USAGE

The Delete command is used to delete parts of text in a HyperCard container. Most often in scripts, it is used to delete text in a card or background field of a particular card. Although it can be used to remove all of the text from a field, it cannot be used to the delete the field itself from the card (you must choose the Field tool and then use *doMenu "Clear Field"* to do this; see DoMenu).

EXAMPLES

delete word 2 of line 3 of field 2

delete last item of field "Street Address"

delete line 3 of bkgnd field 10

delete char 5 of textVar

where *textVar* is a local variable that contains a text string.

NOTE

When using the Delete command to remove lines of text from a field, all of the text up to the last carriage return is deleted; however, the return remains in the field. To remove all lines of text including the carriage returns, use the Put command with the Empty constant, as in

put empty into field 1

Dial

Dials a telephone number through a modem or an audio device that can send tones generated by the Dial command over the telephone lines.

FORM

dial <**source**> [**with modem** [<**modemParameters**>]]

ARGUMENTS

<source>	The HyperCard container that holds the telephone number.
with modem	If this parameter is omitted, HyperCard will generate touch-tone sounds for the number in the source through the Macintosh built-in speaker.
<modem Parameters>	Includes Hayes-compatible modem commands, often referred to as AT commands because they are preceded by *AT*. These commands are used to set up tone or pulse dialing, control the volume of the speaker, or tell the modem how long to stay on the line after the number has been dialed. Refer to your modem documentation for the specific AT commands used by your modem. If the *<modemParameters>* argument is omitted but *dial with modem* is specified in the script, HyperCard uses the AT command "ATS0=0DT".

USAGE ═══════════════════════════════

The Dial command allows you to add automatic telephone-number dialing capabilities to your stacks. With it, you can instruct Hyper-Card to dial any telephone number stored in a container such as a field or the *selection* variable (which contains any string that has been selected by the user).

The Dial command will generate touch-tone sounds through the speaker (if you hold the mouthpiece of the phone to the Macintosh speaker, the sounds from the speaker will sometimes dial the number for you). You can also have the number dialed through a modem attached to your computer. The correct settings for your modem can be specified with the use of AT commands added as the <*modem-Parameters*> part of the *dial with modem* command.

If the telephone number in the <*source*> argument is separated by hyphens (as in 312–555–1765), be sure to enclose the string in a pair of quotation marks ("312–555–1765"). The Dial command will ignore any nonnumeric characters in the container designated as the <*source*> argument.

EXAMPLES ═══════════════════════════

> **dial "(312) 555–7896" with modem "ATDTS7 = 1"**
>
> **dial line 2 of field "Telephone"**
>
> **dial selection**

NOTE ═══════════════════════════════════

The Address stack supplied with the HyperCard software contains a telephone button script using the Dial command that can be adapted to new stacks that you want to equip with automatic telephone dialing. This button makes use of the Phone stack also supplied with HyperCard. This stack allows the user to select the correct settings for his or her computer and telephone system. From the opening card of the Phone stack, you can select the type of dialing and specify dialing prefixes required for local and long-distance calling, as well as local area codes that need not be dialed. If you use the button script from the Address stack, be sure to alert the user to have the Phone stack available when using the auto-dialing button.

Divide

Divides the number in the $<destination>$ by the number in the $<source>$ and puts the answer in the $<destination>$ argument.

FORM

divide <destination> by <source>

ARGUMENTS

$<destination>$ Any HyperCard container such as a field, a variable, or the Message box. The result is stored in the $<destination>$ argument.

$<source>$ Any value or expression that produces a value when evaluated. This value can be stored in any HyperCard container.

USAGE

The Divide command allows you to perform the operation of division in a script. The result of the division is stored in the $<destination>$ argument. This means that the value originally held in this container will be replaced by the result of division. To preserve the two values that are divided, make use of a variable as an intermediate storage container (see the second example that follows).

EXAMPLES

divide field 1 by field 2

If field 1 contains 10 and field 2 contains 2, field 1 will contain 5 after the Divide command is executed.

```
on mouseUp
  put field "Item 1" into tempNum
  divide tempNum by field "Item 2"
  put tempNum into field "Percent of Change"
end mouseUp
```

where *tempNum* is a local memory variable.

NOTE

You can also perform the operation of division in a script by using the / (slash) between two values or two HyperCard containers that hold values, as in the following:

```
put field 1/15 into field "Average"
```

SEE ALSO

Add command
Multiply command
Subtract command

Do

Executes the first line of text in the <*source*> argument as though it were entered as a HyperTalk command in the Script Editor.

FORM

do <**source**>

ARGUMENT

<*source*>   Refers to any HyperCard container that holds a text string, such as a field, a variable, or the Message box. If the <*source*> argument refers to a field that contains multiple lines of text and the line is not specified, the text string in the first line of the field is executed. The text string held by the <*source*> argument must contain a valid HyperTalk command using the correct syntax, otherwise the Do command in the script is ignored.

USAGE

The Do command allows you to store a HyperTalk command in a HyperCard container and have it executed as though it were entered as part of the script being executed. Only one HyperTalk command can be executed by the Do command. To specify the execution of a specific command in a field that has many lines, specify the number of the line that contains the command statement to be executed. If you do not specify the line number as part of the <*source*> argument, HyperCard executes the first line of the field specified.

do line 3 of field 2

If line 3 of field 2 of the card current when the Do command is executed contains the text *doMenu "New Card"*, a new card is added to the stack.

do newCommand

If the local variable named *newCommand* contains the text *go home*, HyperCard goes to the Home Card once this Do command is executed.

DoMenu command

DoMenu

Performs one of the menu options on the HyperCard or Apple menu.

FORM

doMenu <name of menu item>

ARGUMENT

<name of menu item> Refers to the name of the menu option as it appears on the HyperCard or Apple menu when selected with the mouse. You must enter the option name exactly as it appears on either of these menus. When a Hyper-Card menu option includes an ellipsis (...), it must be entered. The name of the menu option must be enclosed in a pair of quotation marks when its name includes spaces (as in *doMenu "New Card"*).

USAGE

The DoMenu command in HyperTalk allows you to have your scripts select and execute HyperCard menu options as though they had been selected from the pull-down menus with the mouse. You can also use the DoMenu command to have a script execute one of the options on the Apple menu such as the Control Panel or Chooser menu options. (*DoMenu "Chooser"* can be used to give the user a chance to choose between using the ImageWriter and the LaserWriter prior to printing cards or a report from a stack; see Open Printing for an example of this.)

EXAMPLES

doMenu "Delete Card"

doMenu "Print Stack..."

doMenu "Chooser"

doMenu menuChoice

where *menuChoice* is a local variable that contains the name of a HyperCard menu option.

NOTE

You do not have to specify the menu containing a particular Hyper-Card option when you use the DoMenu command. However, remember that various menu options are available only when a particular user level is specified or a particular Object tool (the Browse, Button, or Field tool) is used. For example, the Compact Stack menu option is not available on the File menu until the user level is set to at least Painting. Likewise, the Paint, Options, and Patterns menu options are not available unless one of the paint tools is selected. Always make sure that the menu options called for by your DoMenu commands are available before they are executed. If necessary, your script can select the appropriate user level or Object tool before executing the DoMenu commands.

SEE ALSO

Do command

Drag

Drags the mouse from one location on the screen to another. You do not have to include the Click command when using Drag.

FORM

drag from <h,v> **to** <h,v> [**with shiftKey** | **optionKey** | **commandKey**]

ARGUMENTS

<h,v>	Specified by the horizontal and vertical screen coordinates or HyperCard containers that hold such coordinates. The Macintosh screen coordinates are numbered from 0,0 at the upper left corner to 512,342 at the lower right corner. The first pair of *<h,v>* arguments represents the starting position of the cursor; the second pair represents the ending position. You can also specify these arguments by functions or properties that return the appropriate screen coordinates or by HyperCard containers that hold their coordinate numbers.
with shiftKey, *with optionKey,* and *with commandKey*	Use these optional arguments to simulate dragging from a particular location with these keys depressed. When designating the use of more than one of these special keys, separate their names with commas, as in

drag from 25,75 to 50,123 ¬
with shiftKey, optionKey

USAGE

The Drag command allows you to have a script perform dragging on the screen just as you would physically with the mouse. Its use is similar to that of the Click command, except that the Drag command requires both starting and ending screen coordinates. Prior to the addition of the Drag command to a script, you use the Choose command to specify the tool to be used. Most often, this will be one of the paint tools, as this command is useful in scripts that perform drawing on the screen. However, it can also be used when locating and sizing a new or existing text field on the screen.

The optional arguments *with shiftKey*, *with optionKey*, and *with commandKey* can be used with the Drag command. When one of the paint tools has been selected, you can use these keys to perform various enhancements to the drawing being created. For example, when the Polygon tool has been selected, dragging with the Option key draws the figure with the currently selected pattern rather than black. When dragging with the Shift key, the angle of each side of the figure is restricted to multiples of 15 degrees.

EXAMPLES

choose rectangle tool
drag from 35,100 to 70,200

choose oval tool
set centered to true
drag from 100,150 to 125,150 with shiftKey, optionKey

SEE ALSO

Choose command
Click command

Edit Script

Opens the Script Editor of an object to allow you to edit the script of the HyperCard object indicated as the *<object>* argument.

FORM

edit script of *<object>*

ARGUMENT

<object>   Refers to the name of one of the HyperCard objects: stack, card, background, button, or field. The name of the object can be typed in as part of the Edit Script command or designated by a HyperCard container that holds the name of an object.

USAGE

The Edit Script command opens the Script Editor dialog box for the object indicated as the *<object>* argument. This simulates selecting a particular HyperCard object and then clicking on the Script button in the object's dialog box. When HyperTalk executes an Edit Script command, it pauses the execution of any subsequent commands in the script until the Script Editor dialog box is closed (by clicking on either the Cancel or OK button). During this time, the user may examine the script and make any editing changes deemed necessary. All such changes are made by using the standard (manual) editing functions of the Script Editor (see Chapter 1 for information on writing and editing scripts with the Script Editor).

EXAMPLES

> **edit script of button id 345**
>
> **edit script of card "Opening"**
>
> **edit script of bkgnd 1**
>
> **edit script of objectName**

where *objectName* is a local variable that contains the name of the object whose script is to be edited.

NOTE

Remember to differentiate between background and card level buttons and fields when using the Edit Script command to edit these objects. To tell HyperCard that you wish to edit the third card field (as opposed to background field) of a particular card in the stack, add the designation *card*, as in

> **edit script of card field 3 of card "Index"**

SEE ALSO

Script (stack, card, background, field, and button) properties: Chapter 4

Exit

The Exit command causes the program control to jump directly to the end of the message handler, thereby failing to execute any commands that follow the Exit command and precede the End statement.

FORM

    exit <message>

ARGUMENT

    <message>   Refers to the name of the message used in the message handler.

USAGE

The Exit command is used to bypass the standard flow of commands in a message handler. It is used with an If...Then or If...Then...Else construction, which tests for the condition under which the exit to the end of the message handler should take place. The Exit command causes the control of the program to jump directly to the end of the handler. It can be used in the form *exit to HyperCard* to quit HyperTalk completely (thereby exiting from all levels of message handlers).

    The Exit command is versatile. It can be used with the control structures If...Then and Repeat to exit from the control of these structures in the form

    exit if

or

    exit repeat

EXAMPLES

For an example of Exit used in a password protection routine, see
Figure 2.1.

```
on openStack
    ask password
    if it <> field "Password" then
        exit openStack
    else
        set userLevel to 5
        set powerKeys to true
        set blindTyping to true
        show menubar
        go to card "opening"
    end if
end openStack
```

Figure 2.1: Exit command: Example 1

The Exit to HyperCard form can be used in debugging a Hyper-
Talk script.

on errorTrap
  exit to HyperCard
end errorTrap

where *errorTrap* is a user-defined message name containing the commands that check for the program errors to initiate the exit from
HyperTalk.

Find

Finds the characters specified as the <*source*> argument in the stack.

FORMS

find <**source**> [**in** <**field n**>]

find chars <**source**> [**in** <**field n**>]

find word <**source**> [**in** <**field n**>]

ARGUMENTS

<*source*>   Refers to the text string that is to be located in the stack. This string can be typed in (enclosed in a pair of quotation marks) or designated by a HyperCard container that holds the text string.

[*in* <*field n*>]   Using this optional argument restricts the search to a particular field in the stack (as opposed to searching through all of the fields in the stack). For <*field n*>, enter the name, the number, or the ID number of the field or the name of a HyperCard container that holds such information.

USAGE

The HyperTalk Find command works like the Find command on the HyperCard Go menu. It allows you to create a script for locating a particular text string in a stack. When you use the form *find* <*source*>, HyperCard matches the search string entered as the <*source*> argument against the first characters of each word of text in the fields of a card. To have the program find strings of text embedded within words, you must use the *find chars <source>* form of the command. Further, to have the program match the search string against only whole words (those strings separated by spaces), you must use the *find word <source>* form of the command.

The Find command can be used to create the script for a Find button that allows the user to enter the text to search for, and can even restrict the search to a specific field in the cards. For example, you could use the script shown in Figure 2.2 for such a Find button.

```
on mouseUp
    ask "Enter text to search for:"
    put it into searchText
    ask "Enter field name or number to search in:"
    put it into searchField
    if searchText is not empty and ¬
    searchField is empty then
        find searchText
    else
        if searchText is not empty and ¬
        searchField is not empty then
        find searchText in field searchField
        end if
    end if
end mouseUp
```

Figure 2.2: Script for a Find button

There is a drawback to using the Find command in a script as opposed to having the user choose the Find option on the Edit menu. From a script, you cannot use the Return key to have the program locate subsequent matches to the search string in the stack, as is the case when you use the Find option on the Edit menu. As your users will be accustomed to this use of the Return key in Find operations, they may consider the use of a Find button lacking this capability to be frustrating. For this reason, you may want to think twice before you add such a button to your stack, relying instead on the built-in command option.

EXAMPLES

find "New York"

find "Smith" in field "Name"

find chars "start"

find word "start"

NOTE

When a script executes a Find command, the program puts the search string entered as the *<source>* argument into the Message box. This means that you can use the Find option on the Edit menu to locate subequent matches for the search string in the stack as soon as the program locates the first match with the script.

Get

Puts the value of the <*expression*> argument in the *it* variable.

FORM

get <**expression**>

ARGUMENT

<*expression*>   Refers to the name of the property and to the name of the object that the property describes. It can also contain any mathematical expression whose result is numeric.

USAGE

The Get command is most often used to obtain information about a particular HyperCard object. This information can encompass any of the many properties that describe an object's current settings and status. The information obtained by the Get command is automatically stored in the special *it* local variable. You can then have the script branch according to the information stored in the *it* variable. This is done with an If...Then or an If...Then...Else construction that tests the contents of *it* against a particular condition or expression. The outcome of this test then determines what action, if any, the script takes next.

EXAMPLES

get name of this stack

get textFont of field "State"

```
get the loc of card button 4
get style of bkgnd button 2
get 5 ^ 2  – –  puts 25 into the it variable
```

NOTE

The *it* variable used by the Get command is also used by the Ask, Answer, and Read commands. Be sure that you place the information returned by the Get command into another variable, if the *it* variable will be reused by one of these commands as part of the same message handler. Use the Put command to initialize a new variable, as in the following:

```
put it into temp
```

SEE ALSO

Set command
Properties: Chapter 4

Global

Declares a local variable to be a global variable that can be used in other scripts in the same stack and new stacks until you open another application from HyperCard or quit HyperCard.

FORM

   global <**variable name**>

ARGUMENT

   <variable name>   Contains the name of the variable as it was given when created with the Put command. If you wish to declare multiple variables to be global variables with the same Global command, enter them in a list separated by commas (see the last example in the Examples section that follows). You must declare a variable to be global each time you use it in a script.

USAGE

Variables initialized in HyperTalk are *local variables*, meaning they are cleared as soon as the message handler that creates them is finished executing all of its commands. To reuse a variable and preserve the information that it contains, you must use the Global command. This command declares the variable to be a *global variable* that can be used in new scripts, even if those scripts are located in new stacks. Once a variable has been declared to be global, its names and contents can be used until you open a new application from HyperCard (using the Open command) or quit the program.

Use this command anytime you need to reuse the information in a particular variable in scripts other than the one in which it is created.

EXAMPLES

```
on openCard
  global repeatCount
  put 3 into repeatCount
end openCard
```

This Global command declares the *repeatCount* variable to be a global variable. The Put command then initializes it.

```
on mouseUp
  global repeatCount
  beep repeatCount
  answer "Proceed with deletion of card?" ¬
  with "Yes or "No"
  if it is "Yes" then doMenu "Delete Card"
end mouseUp
```

This button script uses the global *repeatCount* variable as the argument of the Beep command. Notice that the Global command is used as the first statement of the message handler. The global repeatCount variable can also be used in other scripts in this stack.

```
global total, ytd, grandTotal
```

This Global command declares all three variables to be global variables.

NOTE

All variables that you define in the Message box are global variables.

Go

Takes you to the card specified in the *<destination>* argument.

FORM

go [**to**] <**destination**>

ARGUMENTS

<destination>   Refers to the name of the stack (omitted if referring to the current stack) and/or the card to be displayed. If the stack is not in the current folder or the top level of the disk, you must specify the path name as part of this argument. If you omit a reference to the card and name only the stack, HyperCard takes you to the first card of the stack specified.

You can specify the card to go to in the *<destination>* argument by its name, number, or ID number in the stack. When referring to a card by number, you can use the cardinal numbers first through tenth (Hyper-Card doesn't know eleventh and up). You can also refer to the card's position in the *<destination>* argument by *first, mid, last, next,* or *previous* (can also be abbreviated to *prev*).

[*to*]   Optional in all uses of the Go command.

USAGE

The Go command is used in scripts to display a new card on the HyperCard screen. The Go command is often used in conjunction with the Visual command to create special visual effects when going from one part of a stack to another or to a new stack altogether.

EXAMPLES

go next card

go to next card of this background

go to card 3 of stack "New Accounts"

go to fifth card

go Address – – opens Address stack and displays card 1

go prev – – takes you to previous card of stack

SEE ALSO

Visual command

Help

Takes the user to the first card of the HyperCard Help stack.

FORM

help

ARGUMENTS

The Help command is one of the few HyperTalk commands that does not require the use of an argument.

USAGE

Putting the Help command in a script is equivalent to selecting the Help option on the Go menu or typing Command-? when using a stack. It takes the user to the first card of the Help stack supplied with HyperCard. From there, the user can examine any information it contains on the use of HyperCard and HyperTalk.

If you wish to add your own custom help to the stack you have created, don't use the HyperTalk Help command. Instead, create a Help or Info button that takes the user to a stack that contains help cards about using your stack whenever the button is clicked on.

EXAMPLES

```
on openStack
    answer "Do you want some info about Hypercard?" ¬
    with "Yes" or "No"
    if it is "Yes" then help
end openStack
```

Hide

Hides the HyperCard menus or the entire screen, the Message box, the Tool or Pattern window, or a specified field or button from view. They are redisplayed with the Show command.

FORM

**hide menubar | card window | <window>
| <field or button>**

ARGUMENTS

menubar   Suppresses the display of the Menu bar at
                     the top of the HyperCard screen.

card window   Suppresses the display of the entire card. If
                     the Message box is displayed when this com-
                     mand is executed, it remains visible. When
                     running HyperCard under MultiFinder, the
                     other windows open are made visible on the
                     desktop.

<window>   Suppresses the display of one of the three
                     HyperCard windows: tool (the Tool menu),
                     pattern (the Patterns palette or menu), and
                     message (the Message box). When hiding the
                     Message box, you can enter the *<window>*
                     argument in a variety of ways:

                             hide message window
                             hide message box
                             hide message
                             hide msg

When hiding either the tool or pattern window, you must enter the name plus the word *window* as the <*window*> argument, as in

hide tool window

<*field or button*>

Suppresses the display of a particular field or button in a card. When specifying the <*field or button*> argument, enter the name, number, or ID number of the field or button or the name of a variable that holds such information. If the field or button to be hidden is at the card level, be sure to add the word *card* to the argument, as in

hide card field 1

USAGE	

In the *hide menubar* form of the command, the display of the Menu bar at the top of the screen with the HyperCard menus is removed from view. Even when the Menu bar is not displayed, the user can still use Command-key alternatives (such as Command-F to select the Find option). However, if the option desired has no Command-key alternate, it cannot be used until the Menu bar is redisplayed with the Show command. You can always redisplay the hidden Menu bar by pressing Command-Space bar.

The *hide card window* form of the Hide command is a new addition to version 1.1 of the program. It allows you to suppress the display of the entire HyperCard screen. When running HyperCard under MultiFinder, you can use this command to display an application running in the window below HyperCard. Note that if the Message box, or the Tool or Patterns menu, is visible on the screen when the script executes the *hide card window* command, they remain visible. To suppress their display, you must also issue the appropriate *hide* <*window*> command.

In addition to using the Hide command to remove the HyperCard windows from view, thus enabling the user to see all of the information on the card, you can also use it to suppress the display of particular fields and buttons. You may use the *hide* <*field or button*> form of the command to create hidden fields and buttons that appear only when a particular action takes place or only when a user requests additional information (by clicking on a button). In such a case, you use the Show command to redisplay the hidden field or button. This makes it possible to annotate information on a particular card without having to go to a new card, while still avoiding cluttering the card with seldom-needed information or seldom-used buttons. (For specific information on how to create hidden fields and buttons, refer to Chapter 12 of *Understanding HyperCard* [SYBEX, 1988].)

EXAMPLES

hide menubar

hide card button 2

hide tool window

hide message

SEE ALSO

Show command

Multiply

Calculates the product of the *<destination>* and *<source>* arguments and puts the answer in the *<destination>* argument.

FORM

multiply <destination> by <source>

ARGUMENTS

<destination>   Any HyperCard container such as a field, a variable, or the Message box. The result is stored in the *<destination>* argument.

<source>   Any value or expression that produces a value when evaluated. This value can be stored in any HyperCard container.

USAGE

The Multiply command allows you to perform the operation of multiplication in a script. The product of the multiplication is stored in the *<destination>* argument. This means that the value originally held in this container will be replaced by the new result. To preserve the two values that are multiplied, use a variable as an intermediate storage container (see the example that follows).

EXAMPLE

```
put field 1 into term
multiply term by 12
put term into field "Number of Payments"
```

NOTE

You can also perform the operation of multiplication in a script by using the * (asterisk) between two values or two HyperCard containers that hold values, as in the following:

put 3.5 * field 2 into field 5

SEE ALSO

Add command
Divide command
Subtract command

Open

Opens a new application from HyperCard.

FORM

open [<**document**> **with**] <**application**>

ARGUMENTS

<*document*>   Refers to the name of the document as it was saved with the application. Specify the full path name if it has not been added to the *Look for Documents in* card in the Home stack and if it is not located at the top level of the disk. If you don't specify a file name for the <*document*> argument, the application opens a new file.

<*application*>   Refers to the name of the application as it appears in the Finder. If the application name uses version numbers or special symbols (such as the trademark or registered trademark), these must added as part of the command. To produce the trademark symbol (™) from the keyboard, press Option-2. To produce the registered trademark symbol (®), press Option-R. To produce the copyright symbol (©), press Option-G. If the location of the application by path name has not been specified in the *Look for Applications in* card in the Home stack, specify the path name as part of the command argument.

You can also open a document or application whose name is entered in HyperCard container (such as a field) by specifying the container as the argument of the *<document>* or *<application>* argument.

USAGE

The Open command allows you to open a new application with a new file or an existing file from a script. Once the script executes the Open command, the program issues a Suspend message that halts the running of HyperCard. As soon as you close the document and quit the application, the system issues a Resume command and HyperCard regains control. In this process, the user is brought back to the place in the stack where he or she was when the Open command was executed.

You can use the Open command to allow the user to start a new program to do work in it or to open a particular document to check information, or even copy information via the Clipboard back into HyperCard. You can also use this command to create a HyperCard finder stack from which you can launch any of the applications that you use on your Macintosh. The HyperCard finder stack can then take the place of the Apple Finder, allowing you to use HyperCard as the base of operations to which you return automatically whenever you finish work with a specific Macintosh application. (See Chapter 15 of *Understanding HyperCard* [SYBEX, 1988] for specific information on creating a HyperCard finder stack.)

EXAMPLES

   open Microsoft Word

   open "Franklin Letter of 9/28" with Microsoft Word

   open dBASE Mac

   open field 2

where *field 2* contains the name of the application to be opened from HyperCard.

NOTE

If you are using MultiFinder instead of the standard Finder, the System will not restart HyperCard and return you to your original place in the stack from which you launched the application with the Open command. However, when running MultiFinder, you only have to click on the window containing your open stack to return to this place.

Open File

The Open File command opens a file for transferring data to and from a HyperCard stack with the Write and Read commands.

FORM

open file <**document**>

ARGUMENT

<*document*> Name of the file to be opened. If the file name uses spaces, enclose it in a pair of quotation marks. The <*document*> argument can also be specified by a HyperCard container that holds the document name. If the document file is not at the top level of the disk or in the same folder as HyperCard, specify the path name as part of the <*document*> argument.

USAGE

The Open File command is used before a Read or Write statement in a script that transfers information between HyperCard and an external file. If the file name specified as the <*document*> argument does not yet exist, the Open File command will create it. Be sure to enter a Close File command with the name of the document file after the Read or Write command (see Read and Write).

EXAMPLES

open file "Accounts 1987"

open file docName

where *docName* is a variable that holds the name of the file to be opened.

SEE ALSO

Close File command
Read command
Write command

Open Printing

Opens a print queue that stores the cards to be printed, which are specified in subsequent Print commands. When the script finds and executes a Close Printing command in the same script, HyperCard sends the print job to the printer.

FORM

open printing [with dialog]
print...
close printing

ARGUMENTS

[*with dialog*]   When you add this optional parameter to the Open Printing command, the program opens the Print Stack dialog box, allowing the user to specify the number of cards per page or to specify one of the available print formats.

close printing   Always add a Close Printing command to the script that contains the Open Printing command. This signals the end of the queue and instructs HyperCard to send the print job to the printer. The Close Printing command is placed after the Print command, which specifies which cards are to be printed as part of the print job.

USAGE

The Open Printing command allows you to set up a print queue, which contains all of the cards to be printed as one job. This allows you to set up a script whereby various cards from different stacks can be printed at one time. You can thereby get around the limitation of the Print Card and Print Stack options on the File menu, which restrict you to printing cards from only one stack at a time.

After entering the Open Printing command in the script, you use the Print command to specify all of the cards to be included in the print job. Be sure to add a Close Printing command after the last Print command; otherwise, the program will not know when to close the queue and the cards in it will not be printed.

EXAMPLE ====================

```
on mouseUp
  open printing with dialog
  doMenu "Chooser"
  go to stack "Sales"
  print all cards
  go to stack "Business Clients"
  print 10
  go last
  print card
  close printing
end mouseUp
```

SEE ALSO ====================

Print command

Pass

Used to pass the original message to the next object in the message inheritance path.

FORM

pass <message>

ARGUMENT

<message>   The name of the HyperCard message to be passed up the hierarchy or the name of a HyperCard container that holds such a message.

USAGE

The Pass command allows a message to continue up the HyperCard hierarchy that would otherwise be trapped and, thus, ignored by subsequent message handlers. For example, when a message handler issues the doMenu message from a script, it traps the doMenu message in that script. If you don't add a *pass doMenu* command to the script, the program will not be able to respond to subsequent doMenu messages placed in other scripts.

When using the Pass command, make sure that you enter it at the end of the script for the message handler. Otherwise, the control will jump beyond the end statement and be sent up the message hierarchy before the commands in the message handler can be executed.

EXAMPLE

See Figure 2.3.

```
        ask "Enter menu option to perform?"
        put it into menuChoice
        .
        .
        .
on doMenu menuChoice
        if menuChoice is "Delete Stack..." then
                ask "Sorry, can't allow that!"
                pass doMenu
        end if
end doMenu
```

Figure 2.3: Example of Pass command

Play

Plays digitized sounds through the Macintosh built-in speaker or an external speaker connected to the computer. You can play musical notes with this command in either the "boing" or "harpsichord" voice.

FORM

play <voice> [tempo <tempo number>] [<notes>]

ARGUMENTS

<voice>	The voices included in HyperCard are "boing," "harpsichord," and "silence." ("Silence" mutes the notes, so you can use this voice if you need pauses or rests.) You can add other voices as external commands. Enter the name of the voice enclosed in a pair of quotation marks.
<tempo number>	The tempo number can be any number between 1 and 500. An andante tempo can be set by using a tempo number of 100. The higher the number, the faster the tempo.
<notes>	The notes are specified by entering their letters or a value equivalent to the note to be played. For instance, middle C is given a note value of 60. Each whole number up or down represents a half-step on the scale. Indicate the use of sharps with # (as in C#) and flats with b (as in Eb) when using the

note letters. Indicate the duration of the note
by using the following abbreviations:

w   whole note

h   half note

q   quarter note

e   eighth note

s   sixteenth note

t   thirty-second note

The octave that the note is to be played in
is indicated by a number. The octave
containing middle C is given the number
4 (if you do not specify an octave number,
the program uses this octave). Octaves 3,
4, and 5 give the best results when played
through the Macintosh built-in speaker.

USAGE

The Play command allows you to add digitized sounds to your
stacks. These sounds can be played through the built-in speaker in
the Macintosh or through an external device. Currently, HyperCard
comes with three voices that can be used with the Play command:
"boing," "harpsichord" (which sounds much more musical), and
"silence," which mutes the notes. To use other voices, you must
include their resources in the Home stack or the stack that contains
the Play command.

Using various voices and sounds, you can add the Play command
to the scripts of buttons in a stack to enhance their functioning. Be
aware that when using the Play command to play music, the list of
musical notes can be very long. In such cases, you must enter a new
Play command at the beginning of each line (including the voice and
tempo parameters). To have the program cease playing a long series
of notes, you can issue the Play command with the stop parameter in
the Message box (*play stop* can also be used in the text of a script).

To use a voice that is created outside of HyperCard, you must
move the sound resource to the stack where it is used. If you move
the sound resource to the Home stack, its sounds will be available for

use in any stack that you create. To move a sound resource to a HyperCard stack, you need to use a resource mover such as ResEdit (Apple's Resource Editor). Once a sound resource has been moved to the Home stack or any other stack, you can use it simply by entering a Play command that uses the name of the sound resource as the <*voice*> argument (see the last example in the following section).

EXAMPLES

    play "harpsichord" tempo 250 "c g# eb3 bb"

    play "boing" "d e f# a"

    play "harpsichord" "55h 61q 82e"

    play "hi"

where "hi" is a digitized sound resource that simulates a voice saying "hi."

Pop Card

Goes to the card most recently marked for retrieval with the Push command.

FORM

pop card [**into** <container>]

ARGUMENTS

<container>   This optional parameter refers to the name of any HyperCard container such as a field, a variable, or the Message box. Indicate the field as the <container> parameter by giving its name, number, or ID number.

[into
<container>]   When you use this parameter, HyperCard places the long name of the card that was last marked for retrieval with the Push command into the container named.

USAGE

The Pop Card command works on the LIFO principle (last in, first out). Therefore, it always retrieves the last card pushed in the special stack created by the Push command. For information on how it is used, see the Push command later in this chapter.

EXAMPLES

pop card

This command takes you to the last card pushed in the stack.

pop card into field 5

This command stores the long name of the last card pushed in the stack in field 5 without taking you to this card.

SEE ALSO

Push command

Print

Prints the current card, a set number of cards, or all cards in the stack. This command can also be used to print a particular document from an external application.

FORMS

print [all | <number> cards | this card]

print <document> with <application>

ARGUMENTS

<number>   Refers to a value or a HyperCard container
                that holds such a value or an expression that
                returns such a value.

<document>   Refers to the name of the file to be printed.
                The name must match the file name used.

<application>   Refers to the name of the application to print
                the file. The name must match the file name
                used. If the application file name uses a ver-
                sion number or special symbol (such as the
                trademark or copyright symbol), these must
                be added to the <application> argument (see
                the Open command for information on how
                to add such special symbols from the key-
                board).

You must specify the path name as part of the <document> and/or <application> argument if either is not at the top level of the disk or in the same folder as HyperCard, and is not already added to the *Look for Documents in* or *Look for Applications in* card in the Home stack.

USAGE ═══════════

The Print command allows you to set up scripts that allow the user to print all or some of the cards in a stack. When used with the Open Printing and Close Printing commands, the Print command adds specified cards to the print queue of the print job. These cards can be located in different stacks (see Open Printing for more information).

The Print command can also be used to print a document created with another application program (see the last two examples in the following section).

EXAMPLES ═══════════

print this card

print 10 cards

print all cards

print "Cost Estimate 4" with Excel

print field 7 with Microsoft Word

where *field 7* holds the name of the document to be printed.

NOTE ═══════════

To allow the user to choose a new printer prior to printing the cards selected, use the command *doMenu "Chooser"* as part of your print script.

SEE ALSO ═══════════

Open Printing command

Push

Marks the current card for later retrieval with the Pop Card command. The last card pushed is the first retrieved by the Pop Card command.

FORM

push [this | recent] card

ARGUMENTS

[*this*]   This optional parameter may be used to designate that the current card is to be pushed in the stack.

[*recent*]   This optional parameter may be used to designate that the most recently viewed card (the card before the current card) is to be pushed in the stack.

USAGE

The Push command marks the current card for later retrieval by adding it to a special stack (not to be confused with the HyperCard stack). From this stack, only the last, or top, card can be retrieved with the Pop command. When HyperCard receives multiple Push commands without an intervening Pop Card command, the cards continue to be added to this stack. As the program executes successive Pop Card commands, cards in the stack move to the top.

You can use the Push command with the Pop Card command to make it easy for the user to return to a previously viewed card. When you want to mark a card for later retrieval with the Pop Card command, use the Push command immediately before the command that takes the user to a new place in the stack (see the example that follows).

If you provide a Return button in the stack that contains a Pop Card command, the user can then click on it to return to whatever card was last pushed in the stack. This will take the user back to the card that was last viewed, provided that HyperCard does not receive another *push card* message before the Return button is used.

EXAMPLE

```
on mouseUp
  push this card
    go to card ID 4567 in stack "Clients"
end mouseUp
```

SEE ALSO

Pop Card command

Put

Puts the contents of the *<source>* argument before, into, or after the container specified as the *<destination>*.

put <**source**> **before** | **into** | **after** <**destination**>

<source>   Refers to the text or expression, or a Hyper-Card container that holds such information. If the text to be placed in the *<source>* argument contains spaces, it must be enclosed in a pair of quotation marks.

<destination>   Refers to the HyperCard container that is to hold the information specified for the *<source>* argument. This container can be a field, a variable, or the Message box (in fact, if the *<destination>* argument is omitted, HyperCard automatically puts the *<source>* into the Message box). This container can also be a chunk expression that refers to a specific part of the information in one of these other containers.

The operative words *before*, *into*, and *after* tell the program where to place the information specified in the *<source>* argument:

into   Replaces the contents of the *<destination>* with the *<source>* information.

before	Joins the *<source>* information to that in the *<destination>* immediately before the place indicated by the *<destination>* argument.
after	Joins the *<source>* information to that in the *<destination>* immediately after the place indicated by the *<destination>* argument.

USAGE

The Put command is a versatile command that allows you to place information in any of the HyperCard containers. You can use it to replace or add to the contents of a particular field. Often, you will use it to initialize a local variable by placing the result of an expression or specific text into it. It can also be used with the Empty constant to clear out the contents of the HyperCard container.

You can use any chunk expression to add text to any part of an existing text string. The Put command allows you to place the new information before or after the existing text (when used with the *into* operative word, the new text replaces the existing text).

You can also use an expression as the *<source>* argument. This expression can be any HyperTalk function or mathematical expression that can be evaluated by the program. Only the result of such an expression will be placed into the designated container. To place the actual mathematical expression (as opposed to the result) into a container, enclose it in a pair of quotation marks, as in

put "4*25 – 25" into field 3

In this example, the text string 4*25 – 25 replaces the existing contents of field 3. Because the expression is enclosed in quotation marks, the result of 75 is not placed in this field.

EXAMPLES

put sum into field "Total"

put it into field 4

put the long date into dateVar

put 3*5/6.4 into newValue
put "average" after word 3 of field 5
put field 3 – 100 before last item of tempVal
put "See you later!"

places the text *See you later!* into the Message box.

SEE ALSO	

Empty constant: Chapter 5

Read

Imports data from an external file into a HyperCard stack and stores the data in the *it* local variable.

read from file <**fileName**> **until** <**character**>

read from file <**fileName**> **for** <**number of bytes**>

<*fileName*>	Refers to the name of the file from which the data is imported. It must match the name of the file given as the argument of the Open File command. Include the full path name if the file is not located at the top level of the disk or in the same folder and has not yet been added to the *Look for Documents in* card in the Home stack.
<*character*>	Refers to the name of the constant given to the character. Usually, the Tab, Return, or Space constant is used.
<*number of bytes*>	Refers to a value or a container that holds such a value, representing the total number of bytes that are to be imported from the file into the *it* variable.

The Read command is used to copy data from an existing text file into HyperCard. The data transferred from the file is stored in the *it* local variable. From there, it can be stored in a particular field of a card by using the Put command. The Read command must be preceded by a Open File command and followed with a Close File command, which specify the name of the file whose text is to be imported. The file whose data you want to import into a HyperCard stack must have been saved in the text-only format (that is, as an ASCII file).

The type of file to be imported determines the character to be used as the *<character>* argument in that form of the command. If you are importing data from a spreadsheet or database program, you will want to use the tab character because individual data items are separated by tabs in these files. When importing data from a word processing document, you will want to use the return character. In such a case, make sure that the HyperCard field will be able to accommodate all of the text up to a return character, as this character is used to separate paragraphs of text that can be quite long.

EXAMPLE

The example in Figure 2.4 gives you a sample script for an Import button that can be added to your stacks. It uses two Repeat constructions to add new cards to an existing stack and to import the data up

```
on mouseUp
    ask "Enter name of file to import text from?"
    if it is empty then exit mouseUp
    put it into importDoc
    open file importDoc
    repeat
        doMenu "New Card"
        repeat with field# = 1 to the number of fields
            read from file importDoc      until tab
            if it is empty then   -- end of file
                if field# = 1 then doMenu "Delete Card"
                close file importDoc
                exit mouseUp
            end if
            put it into field field#
        end repeat
    end repeat
end mouseUp
```

Figure 2.4: Example of Read command

to a tab character into each field of the new cards. This can be used in any stack that imports data from a spreadsheet or database where tabs separate data items. Be sure that the stack to receive the data already exists and contains at least one card with all of the fields required to accept the incoming information.

SEE ALSO

Close File command
Open File command
Write command
Return, Space, and Tab constants: Chapter 5

Reset Paint

Resets the options in the painting program's Options menu and the characteristics of the paint text back to their default settings.

FORM

reset paint

ARGUMENTS

The Reset Paint command requires no arguments. When it is used in a script, the following default settings are put into effect:

grid to false
lineSize to 1
filled to false
centered to false
multiple to false
multiSpace to 1
pattern to 12 (black)
brush to 8 (medium dot)
polySides to 4 (square)
textAlign to left
textFont to Geneva
textSize to 12
textHeight to 16
textStyle to Plain

USAGE

The Reset Paint command gives you a quick and efficient way of resetting all of the painting program options back to their defaults.

You can use it at the end of a script that modifies some of these settings when drawing, to ensure that painting program settings are returned to their orginal values before the painting program is used again.

EXAMPLE

See Figure 2.5.

```
on mouseUp
        choose rectangle tool
        set filled to true
        set pattern to 11
        set lineSize to 2
        set centered to true
        drag from 120,200 to 180,295
        choose text tool
        set textSize to 18
        set textFont to New York
        set textStyle to bold
        click at 150,210
        type "Greetings!"
        reset paint
end mouseUp
```

Figure 2.5: Example of Reset Paint command

Send

Sends a message to an object not in the regular message hierarchy of the current script.

FORM

send <**message**> **to** <**target**>

ARGUMENTS

<*message*> Refers to the name of a HyperCard message or a container that holds the name of such a message. The message must be either one word, or several words joined by an underscore (_).

<*target*> Refers to the HyperCard object that is to receive the message. This can be HyperCard, Home, the stack, card, background, button, or field. When the target is a card, button, or field, you can refer to it by name, number, or ID number. If it is not located in the current stack, be sure to include a reference to it by name.

USAGE

The Send command allows you to send a system message or a message of your own making to a specific HyperCard object. This enables you to send the message to an object that is not directly in line in the message hierarchy (see Chapter 1 for details on the HyperCard message hierarchy and for more information on message handlers). The Send command can be used to automate many functions within a script. By sending a MouseUp message when a certain action takes place (such as closing a field or opening a stack), you can have a button activated without having to use the Click command.

EXAMPLES

send closefield to button "Next"

send quit to HyperCard

on openCard
   send mouseUp to button "New Card"
end openCard

When you go to the card that contains this message handler, it automatically sends a MouseUp message to the button whose function is to add a new card to the stack.

Set

Sets the property of an object to a new value.

FORM

set <property> of <object> to <value>

ARGUMENTS

<property>   Refers to the name of the property that you want to set. This can be the name of any HyperCard property that can be set (some properties cannot be changed with the Set command; see Chapter 4 for specific examples).

<object>   Refers to the name of the object that owns the property to be changed with the Set command. As you can see from the list of properties in Chapter 4, the HyperCard objects of stack, card, background, button, and field each have many properties that can be modified with the Set command. In addition, the HyperCard windows (tool, pattern, and message) and the painting program all have properties that can be changed with the Set command.

<value>   Refers to the new setting you can assign to the property of the object. What values are accepted depend upon the property in question. In some cases, the *<value>* argument will be simply true or false; in others it will be a new number representing a new setting;

and in still others it will be a text string
(which, if it includes spaces, must be
enclosed in quotation marks).

USAGE

The Set command allows you to change the settings of a multitude
of properties associated with specific HyperCard objects. It simulates the use of the dialog boxes associated with particular Hyper-
Card menu options, which allow you to select new values for a
particular aspect of the program. The Set command allows you to
control most of the program settings from within a script.

EXAMPLES

set the textFont of field 1 to Chicago

set style of card button 3 to shadow

set visible of tool window to true

set icon of button 2 to "Sort"

set name of card to "Housekeeping"

SEE ALSO

Properties: Chapter 4

Show

Redisplays the HyperCard Menu bar or card window, or any HyperCard window, field, or button that has been previously hidden with the Hide command. It can also be used to have HyperCard browse through a set number of cards or all of the cards in the current stack.

show menubar | **card window** | **<window>**
| **<field or button>** [**at <location>**]

show [**<number>** | **all**] **cards**

menubar	Redisplays the Menu bar at the top of the HyperCard screen.
card window	Redisplays the entire HyperCard card window.
<window>	Redisplays one of the three HyperCard windows: tool (the Tool menu), pattern (the Patterns palette or menu), or message (the Message box). When showing the Message box, you can enter the *<window>* argument in a variety of ways:

> **show message window**
> **show message box**
> **show message**
> **show msg**

When showing either the tool or pattern window, you must enter the name plus the word *window* as the <*window*> argument, as in

show tool window

<*field or button*> Redisplays a particular field or button in a card. When specifying the <*field or button*> argument, enter the name, number, or ID number of the field or button or the name of a variable that holds such information. If the field or button to be shown is at the card level, be sure to add the word *card* to the argument, as in

show card field 1

[*at* <*location*>] This optional argument is used to relocate the position of the card window (only if HyperCard is used on an external monitor—the card window cannot be moved on the 9-inch built-in screen), or a HyperCard window, button, or field on the screen. Enter the <*location*> by giving the number of the horizontal and vertical screen coordinates, separated by commas. With buttons or fields, these coordinates refer to the center of the objects. With HyperCard windows, these coordinates refer to the upper left corner of the window.

[<*number*>] The value or an expression that results in a value representing the number of succeeding cards to be displayed on the screen.

[all] Displays all of the cards in the stack, starting with the next card and stopping at the card right before the card current when the *show all* statement is executed.

USAGE

The Show command can be used in scripts to redisplay various objects that have been hidden with the Hide command. It can also be used to relocate a HyperCard card on the screen. By adding the [*at* <*location*>] parameter to the Show command, you can have the script move the window to a new position. Note that it is not necessary to have previously hidden the window (with the Hide command) before using the Show command to move the window to a new screen position. You can move the card window, tool window, pattern window, message window, or a particular button or field. However, you cannot use the Show command to reposition the HyperCard Menu bar.

In addition to using the Show command to redisplay a hidden window and/or relocating it on the screen, you can use the Show command to have the script browse through a group or all of the cards in a stack, displaying cards one at a time. The user can stop the browsing operation initiated with the *show cards* form at any time by pressing the Command-period key combination. If you omit the optional <*number*> argument or all parameters from the *show cards* form, the program browses through and displays all of the cards in the current stack.

EXAMPLES

   show menubar

   show tool window

   show message

   show field "Notes"

   show 10 cards

   show all cards

NOTE

The *show card window* form of the Show command was added in version 1.1. If you are using version 1.0, this command is not available. *Show card window* is most useful if you are using HyperCard on a Macintosh equipped with an external monitor that can show multiple windows on the screen. It is particularly useful if HyperCard is running under MultiFinder. However, when designing stacks for distribution, you cannot count on the user having either an external monitor or using MultiFinder. Therefore, you should use this command sparingly in the scripts you write.

SEE ALSO

Hide command

Sort

Sorts the cards in a stack in ascending or descending order by the field or the expression specified.

FORM

sort [ascending | descending] [text | numeric | international | dateTime] by <field or expression>

ARGUMENTS

[*ascending* | *descending*]	Ascending order is from lowest to highest for numbers and A–Z for letters. Descending order is from highest to lowest for numbers and Z–A for letters. If this parameter is not specified in the Sort command, the program sorts in ascending order.
[*text*]	The text sort follows the ASCII sort order, that is, the order of the ASCII character set (see Appendix A). It is used when the field to be sorted on contains alphanumeric text. If you do not specify a sort type as part of the Sort command, the program uses the text sort.
[*numeric*]	The numeric sort arranges numbers correctly according to value rather than position in the ASCII character set. This order does not sort alphanumeric text or text that is composed of nonnumeric characters only.
[*international*]	The international sort order is used with foreign alphabets, which use accent marks and ligatures.

[*dateTime*]	The dateTime sort order is used when sorting on a field that contains only dates or times. When used with dates in ascending order, the program sorts the cards from oldest to most recent date.
<*field or expression*>	When specifying the field that the cards are to be sorted on, you can designate an entire field or just a part of it (with a chunk expression) that it is to be sorted on. You can also enter an expression that involves a calculation as the sorting key.

USAGE

If you want to sort the cards in the stack, you must use the Sort command in a HyperTalk script, as HyperCard does not provide a menu option for sorting. The Sort command gives you much flexibility in determining the order in which the stack is ultimately to be arranged. To begin sorting, designate as the <*field or expression*> argument a key field or part of a field whose contents determine the arrangement of the cards in the stack.

You can also specify an expression involving fields whose calculated result determines the final sort of the cards. To do so, sort by the difference between two fields (see the last example in the section that follows).

If the field contains only values, specify sorting with the optional [*numeric*] parameter. If the field contains only dates or times, specify sorting by the [*dateTime*] parameter. Text sorting is the default used when the field contains alphanumeric text or numbers such as zip codes that are not used in calculations.

EXAMPLES

sort by field 2

sort by last item of line 4 of field "Address"

sort numeric by field "Cost"

sort descending dateItem by field "Date Entered"
sort descending numeric by field "Price" − field "Cost"

This example uses a calculated result to determine the sorting order.

Subtract

Subtracts the value in the <*source*> from the value in the <*destination*> and places the answer in the <*destination*> argument.

FORM

   subtract <source> from <destination>

ARGUMENTS

   <*source*>   Any value or expression that produces a
                     value when evaluated. This value can be
                     stored in any HyperCard container.

   <*destination*>   Any HyperCard container such as a field, a
                     variable, or the Message box. The result is
                     stored in the <*destination*> argument.

USAGE

The Subtract command allows you to perform the operation of subtraction in a script. The result of the subtraction is stored in the <*destination*>. This means that the value originally held in this container will be replaced by the calculated difference. To preserve the two values that are to be subtracted, make use of a variable as an intermediate storage container (see the example that follows).

EXAMPLE

   **put field 1 into newNumber
   subtract field 2 from newNumber
   put newNumber into field 3**

NOTE

You can also perform the operation of subtraction in a script by
using a − (hyphen) between two values or two HyperCard containers that hold values, as in

put field 3 − 250.12 into field 7

SEE ALSO

Add command
Multiply command
Divide command

Type

Types the text that you enter as the <*source*> argument into a container such as a field or variable.

FORM

type <**source**> [**with shiftKey** | **optionKey** |
commandKey]

ARGUMENT

<*source*>   Refers to the text or a HyperCard container
                 that holds the text to be typed at the current
                 position of the flashing text insertion pointer.
                 If you directly enter the text as the <*source*>
                 argument and it includes spaces, you must
                 enclose it in quotation marks.

USAGE

The Type command simulates typing on the screen. To determine
the place where the typing is done, this command must be preceded
by a Click command. (Also, make sure that the Browse tool has been
selected prior to the execution of the Type command.)

The Type command differs from the Put command, which can
also be used to enter text somewhere on the HyperCard screen.
When text is entered with the Type command, the user can see it
appear letter by letter. When text is entered with the Put command,
it appears all at once. The Type command can be used effectively in
educational applications to demonstrate to the user how text is
entered in a particular HyperCard container, such as a field or the
Ask command dialog box.

EXAMPLE

```
on mouseUp
  choose browse tool
  click at loc field 3
  type "Check calendar and schedule meeting."
end mouseUp
```

NOTE

Note that the use of the optional *with shiftKey*, *with optionKey*, and *with commandKey* parameters does not cause the program to type the characters and symbols that would be produced if these keys were manually depressed, as you type the characters specified in the <*source*> argument.

SEE ALSO

Choose command
Click command
Put command

Visual

Specifies a particular visual effect to be used at the next Go or Find command.

FORM
---

visual [effect] <name of effect> [speed]
[to black | white | gray]

ARGUMENTS

[*effect*]	The Visual command can be entered as *visual* or *visual effect* followed by the name of the effect.
<*name of effect*>	The visual effects available in HyperCard that can be entered as the <*name of effect*> argument of the Visual command are as follows:

> dissolve
> checkerboard
> venetian blinds
> zoom open, zoom close, zoom in, zoom out
> iris open, iris close
> barn door open, barn door close
> wipe left, wipe right, wipe up, wipe down
> scroll left, scroll right, scroll up, scroll down

[*speed*]	This optional parameter is added by entering one of the following adverbs, which

describe the relative rate at which the
visual effect takes place:

fast
very fast
slow, slowly
very slow, very slowly

[*to black* | *white* | *gray*] These optional parameters can be used to specify that the particular visual effect is to go to either a black, white, or gray background before displaying the card.

USAGE

The Visual command can be used to add interesting visual transitions when going from one card to another in a stack. When adding a visual effect with this command, you place the Visual command before the Go or Find command that takes the user to a new card. This command can also be used with the Pop Card command to add a visual effect when retrieving the last card pushed in the stack. You can add multiple visual effects to a transition by adding Visual commands one after the other, each on its own line of the Script Editor.

EXAMPLES

visual effect wipe left slowly

visual effect iris open fast

visual effect checkerboard very slowly

visual effect scroll right

visual dissolve to black

Wait

Pauses the execution of the commands in a script for a set period of time or until a particular condition is met or ceases to exist.

FORMS

wait [for] <**number of ticks**>

wait [for] <**number**> **seconds**

wait until <**true or false expression**>

wait while <**true or false expression**>

ARGUMENTS

<*number of ticks*> or <*number*>	Refers to a value or a HyperCard container that holds a value, or to an expression that yields such a value. When the word *seconds* is not specified after the value or container name, the program is paused for the number of ticks rather than seconds.
<*true or false expression*>	Refers to a Boolean expression that, once evaluated, yields either true or false. Generally, this expression represents a mouse or keyboard function that returns true or false.

USAGE

The Wait command is used to pause the program either for a specified period of time, until a certain condition is met, or while it is in effect. The pause introduced with the Wait command is most often used to pause the browsing of cards to allow the user time to digest the information. It can be used with the Show command when

browsing cards or between various Go commands that take the user
to a new place in the stack.

The Wait command has two forms. In the first, you specify the
time period that program execution is to be paused. The time period
can be specified in seconds or ticks (with one tick equal to about one-
sixtieth of a second). In the second form, program execution is
paused conditionally. When you use the *wait until* syntax, the
program is paused until the specified expression is met. When
you use the *wait while* syntax, it is paused until the specified
expression passes.

EXAMPLES

wait for 30 – – 30 ticks = 30/60 (½) second

wait 3 seconds

wait until mouse is down

wait while mouse is up

Write

Writes the text specified in the *<source>* argument into a Macintosh text (ASCII) file.

FORM

write <source> to file <fileName>

ARGUMENTS

<source>   Refers to the text or the name of the Hyper-Card container that holds the text to be transferred to the new text file. It can also refer to the name of a HyperTalk constant such as Tab, Space, or Return that indicates its character is to be written to the new file.

<fileName>   Refers to the name of the file that is to receive the text in the HyperCard stack. If the file name contains spaces, be sure to enclose it in quotation marks.

USAGE

The Write command allows you to write scripts that transfer text stored in HyperCard fields into a text (ASCII) file for use with other Macintosh application programs. It must be preceded by an Open File command and followed by a Close File command as part of the same message handler.

When writing HyperCard text field information to a new file, you must decide what character you want to use to delimit the text stored in each separate field. If the new file is to be used with a spreadsheet or database management program, use the tab character by entering the Tab constant (see the example in the section that follows). If you want to use the file with a word processor, you may want to have a space or return character entered after the text from each Hyper-Card field is written to the new file. To do this, enter either the Space or Return constant in the script.

EXAMPLE

See Figure 2.6.

```
on mouseUp
     ask "Name of file to write to?"
     if it is empty then exit mouseUp
     put it into writeTo
     open file writeTo
     go to first card
     repeat for the number of cards
          repeat with fieldCount = 1 to the number of cards
               write field fieldCount to file writeTo
               write tab to file writeTo
          end repeat
          go to next card
     end repeat
     close file writeTo
end mouseUp
```

Figure 2.6: Example of Write command

SEE ALSO

Close File command
Open File command
Read command
Return, Space, and Tab constants: Chapter 5

CHAPTER 3

The HyperTalk Functions

The HyperTalk language includes a wide variety of functions. A function differs from a command in that it calculates or returns a result rather that initiating a particular action in the script. With few exceptions, the HyperTalk functions require the use of arguments to further define the desired result.

When a particular function requires only a single argument (as opposed to a list of arguments), you have a choice between two alternate forms. For example, the function Sqrt, which calculates the square root of the <*number*> entered as its argument, can be entered as either

the sqrt of <number>

or

sqrt(<number>**)**

Although the first form is more English-like and the second form is shorter and quicker to enter, either form will do the job. Just remember that when using the second form, the argument must be set off with a pair of parentheses.

The functions in HyperTalk are varied. They run the gamut from string functions, such as Length and Offset, to arithmetical functions, such as Sqrt and Ln. You will also note a group of functions whose purpose is to report on the status of the mouse or one of the special keyboard keys (the Shift, Option, and Command keys). These functions return logical results—either true or false, expressed as *up* or *down*. In this way, they resemble the HyperTalk properties (the subject of Chapter 4) much more than they do the standard HyperTalk functions. Table 3.1 summarizes the HyperTalk functions.

DATE AND TIME FUNCTIONS

the abbr date

the abbrev date

the abbreviated date

the date

the long date

the long time

the seconds

the secs

the short time

the ticks

the time

FINANCIAL FUNCTIONS

annuity(<periodic rate>, <number of periods>)

compound(<periodic rate>, <number of periods>)

MATH FUNCTIONS

abs(<number>), the abs of <number>

atan(<angle in radians>), the atan of <angle in radians>

Table 3.1: HyperTalk Functions by Category

average(<number list>)

cos(<angle in radians>), the cos of <angle in radians>

exp(<number>), the exp of <number>

exp1(<number>), the exp1 of <number>

exp2(<number>), the exp2 of <number>

ln(<number>), the ln of <number>

ln1(<number>), the ln1 of <number>

log2(<number>), the log2 of <number>

max(<number list>)

min(<number list>)

random(<number>), the random of <number>

round(<number>), the round of <number>

sin(<angle in radians>), the sin of <angle in radians>

sqrt(<number>), the sqrt of <number>

tan(<angle in radians>), the tan of <angle in radians>

trunc(<number>), the trunc of <number>

MISCELLANEOUS FUNCTIONS

[the] number of cards | buttons | fields

[the] number of <components> in <container>

the param of <number>, param (<number>)

the paramCount

the params

the result

Table 3.1: HyperTalk Functions by Category (continued)

the sound

the target

the tool

MOUSE AND KEY FUNCTIONS

the clickLoc

the commandKey, the cmdKey

the mouse

the mouseClick

the mouseH

the mouseLoc

the mouseV

the optionKey

the shiftKey

STRING FUNCTIONS

charToNum(<character>), the charToNum of
<character>

length(<source>), the length of <source>

numToChar(<number>), the numToChar of
<number>

offset(<text1>,<text2>)

value(<expression>), the value of <expression>

Table 3.1: HyperTalk Functions by Category (continued)

This chapter gives you an alphabetical reference for all the built-in
HyperTalk functions. You should, however, be aware that the functions
within this language are not static. If you do not find a ready-made function for a calculation that you need to use often in the scripts you write,
you can create your own. This ability to create your own functions in
the language is akin to the ability to create your own message handlers,
and thereby extend the command language. (To find out how you go
about defining your own functions, refer to Building Your Own Functions in the section on Using the Arithmetic Operators in Chapter 1.)

Abs

Returns the absolute value of the number entered as the argument.

FORMS

abs(<number>)

the abs of <number>

ARGUMENT

<number>   Refers to a value or a HyperCard container
               that holds a value. It can also refer to an
               expression that results in a value entered
               directly as the argument or held in a con-
               tainer named as the argument.

USAGE

The Abs function yields the absolute value of a number. This converts the value to positive if it has a negative sign and leaves it
unchanged if it is currently positive. Use this function in scripts
where only positive values should be used.

EXAMPLES

abs(−17)

returns 17.

abs(average(−2, −6.7,1.5))

returns 2.4, which is the absolute value of the average of these three numbers.

the abs of temp

where *temp* is a local variable that contains a number or an expression.

Annuity

Returns the present value of a single payment of an annuity.

FORM

annuity(<periodic rate>, <number of periods>)

ARGUMENTS

<periodic rate>	Refers to the value representing the interest during the term. It can be entered as a value, as an expression that yields a value, or as the name of a container that holds such a value or expression.
<number of periods>	Refers to the value representing the term of the annuity. It too can be entered as a value, as an expression that yields a value, or as the name of a container that holds such a value or expression.

USAGE

You can use the Annuity function to calculate the present or future value of a single payment of an annuity. It uses the formula

$$\frac{1 - (1 + r)^{(-n)}}{r}$$

where r is the periodic rate and n is the number of payments.

EXAMPLES

  annuity(.12,36)

  annuity(field "Rate",field "Term")

NOTE

The arguments of the Annuity function can only be entered enclosed in parentheses. HyperCard will *not* accept the form

  the annuity of <periodic rate>,<number of periods>

because multiple arguments are required.

SEE ALSO

  Compound function

Atan

Returns the arctangent of the angle specified.

Forms

atan(<angle in radians>)

the atan of <angle in radians>

ARGUMENT

<angle in radians>   Refers to the number of radians or an expression that yields this number. This value or expression can be entered directly as the argument or indirectly by entering the name of the HyperCard container that holds such a value or expression.

USAGE

The Atan function is used to calculate the arctangent of an angle expressed in radians. To convert an angle expressed in degrees to radians for use with this function, multiply the number by Pi (the constant that holds the value of π to 20 places) and then divide it by 180 (see the first example in the following section).

EXAMPLES

atan(35 * pi/180)

where *pi/180* converts the 35° angle to radians.

atan(acuteAngle)

where *acuteAngle* is a local variable that contains the angle in radians.

SEE ALSO

Cos function
Sin function
Tan function
Pi constant: Chapter 5

Average

Returns the average (mean) of the list of numbers entered as the argument of the function.

FORM

average(<number list>)

ARGUMENT

<*number list*>   Refers to the listing of values to be averaged, separated by commas. You can also enter expressions or the names of HyperCard containers that hold values or expressions.

USAGE

The Average function gives you the mean value from among those entered in the <*number list*> argument. The average is calculated by totaling the values in the number list and dividing by the number of values in the list.

EXAMPLES

average(15,23.2,7*5.12,56)

returns 32.51, which is the average of the four values (the calculated value of 7*5.12 is counted as one value).

average(field 1,field 3, field 5)

NOTE

The *<number list>* argument of the Average function must be entered enclosed in parentheses. HyperCard will *not* accept the form

the average of 3,4,5

because multiple values are required in the argument.

CharToNum

Converts the character specified as the function argument into its equivalent ASCII code decimal number.

FORMS

charToNum(<character>)

the charToNum of <character>

ARGUMENT

<character>   Refers to the character typed from the keyboard and enclosed in quotation marks, or to the name of a container that holds the character.

USAGE

The CharToNum function returns the ASCII decimal code number for any character that can be entered from the keyboard. This character must be enclosed in quotation marks. The function yields the value representing the decimal code for the character according to the ASCII character code chart.

EXAMPLES

charToNum("A") – – returns ASCII code 65

the charToNum of "a" – – returns ASCII code 97

NOTE

To return the ASCII value for a space (32) with the CharToNum function, enter a space (by pressing the Space bar) enclosed in quotation marks as the argument of the function.

SEE ALSO

NumtoChar function

ClickLoc

Returns the screen location of the most recent click of the mouse.

FORM

the clickLoc

ARGUMENTS

The ClickLoc function does not require any arguments.

USAGE

The ClickLoc function returns the horizontal and vertical screen coordinates of the position where the mouse was last clicked before the function is evaluated. The horizontal and vertical screen coordinate values are separated by commas. These values represent the position of the last mouse click by the number of pixels across and down from the upper left corner of the HyperCard screen, which has the screen coordinates of 0,0.

This function can be used effectively in scripts where the position of the last mouse click determines a starting or ending position for drawing on the screen.

EXAMPLES

if item 2 of the clickLoc > 100 then
show message box at 20,50
end if

where item 2 is the vertical screen coordinate.

put the clickLoc into startPos

where *startPos* is a local variable.

SEE ALSO

MouseLoc function

CommandKey

Tells you whether the Command key is depressed.

FORMS

the commandKey

the cmdKey

ARGUMENTS

The CommandKey function does not require any arguments.

USAGE

The CommandKey function returns *down* if the Command key is depressed when the message handler that contains this function is executed. It returns *up* if this key is not depressed at the time. It is most often used in an If...Then construction to determine what action the script is to take depending upon whether the key is down or up.

EXAMPLE

```
on mouseUp
  if the commandKey is down then exit mouseUp
  .
  .
  .
end mouseUp
```

SEE ALSO

OptionKey function
ShiftKey function

Compound

Returns the compound interest at a particular interest rate for a specific number of periods.

FORM

compound(<periodic rate>, <number of periods>)

ARGUMENTS

<periodic rate>	Refers to the value representing the interest during the term. It can be entered as a value, as an expression that yields a value, or as the name of a container that holds such a value or expression.
<number of periods>	Refers to the value representing the term of the annuity. It too can be entered as a value, as an expression that yields a value, or as the name of a container that holds such a value or expression.

USAGE

The Compound function can be used to calculate the compound interest for an annuity. It uses the formula

$$(1 + r)^{(n)}$$

where r is the periodic rate and n is the number of payments.

EXAMPLES

compound(.09,48)

compound(field "Rate",field "Term")

SEE ALSO

Annuity function

Cos

Returns the cosine of the angle specified.

FORMS

cos(<angle in radians>)

the cos of <angle in radians>

ARGUMENT

*<angle
in radians>*   Refers to the number of radians or to an
expression that yields this number. This
value or expression can be entered directly as
the argument or indirectly by entering the
name of the HyperCard container that holds
such a value or expression.

USAGE

The Cos function is used to calculate the cosine of an angle
expressed in radians. To convert an angle expressed in degrees to
radians for use with this function, multiply the number by Pi (the
constant that holds the value of π to 20 places) and then divide it by
180 (see the first example in the following section).

EXAMPLES

cos(25.5 * pi/180)

where *pi/180* converts the 25.5° angle to radians.

cos(acuteAngle)

where *acuteAngle* is a local variable.

SEE ALSO

Atan function
Sin function
Tan function
Pi constant: Chapter 5

Date

Returns the current date in a variety of formats, depending upon the form specified.

the date	– – **12/28/89**
the long date	– – **Thursday, December 28, 1989**
the abbreviated date	– – **Thu, Dec 28, 1989**
the abbrev date	
the abbr date	

The Date function requires no arguments.

The Date function returns the current date as kept by the Macintosh internal clock. The form of the function that you use determines how the current date returned is formatted. The examples in the following section demonstrate the different formats.

When using *the date* (or one of the other Date function forms) in a calculation, convert the result of the function into seconds using the Convert command (see Convert in Chapter 2 for more information).

Assume that the current date is November 24, 1989. If you enter

put the date into currentDate

in a script, the text *11/24/89* will be placed in the currentDate variable.
If you enter

put the long date into currentDate

the text *Friday, November 24, 1989* will be placed in the currentDate variable.
If you enter

put the abbrev date into currentDate

the text *Fri, Nov 24, 1989* will be placed in the currentDate variable.

NOTE

You must preface the Date function with the word *the*. For example,
HyperCard will not understand the function if you just enter

date

in a script.

SEE ALSO

Time function
Convert command: Chapter 2

Exp

Returns the natural exponent—that is, the exponent in base *e*—of the
<*number*> specified.

FORMS

exp(<number>)

the exp of <number>

ARGUMENT

<*number*>   Refers to a value or an expression that results in
                    a value. It can also refer to a HyperCard con-
                    tainer that holds such a value or expression.

USAGE

The Exp function calculates the exponential of the number specified
as the argument. The value returned by this function represents the
constant *e* (2.7182818) raised to the power of the number specified
as the argument.

EXAMPLES

exp(3.5)

which returns the value of $e^{3.5}$.

the exp of tempVar

where *tempVar* is a local variable.

SEE ALSO

Exp1 function
Exp2 function

Exp1

Returns the natural exponent—that is, the exponent in base *e*—of the
<*number*> specified, minus 1.

FORMS

exp1(<number>)

the exp1 of <number>

ARGUMENT

<*number*>   Refers to a value or an expression that results in
                    a value. It can also refer to a HyperCard con-
                    tainer that holds such a value or expression.

USAGE

The Exp1 function calculates the exponential of the number specified as the argument, minus 1. The value returned by this function
represents one less than the constant *e* (2.7182818) raised to the
power of the number specified as the argument, or

$$e^n - 1$$

where *n* is the argument.

EXAMPLES

exp1(6)

which returns the value of $e^6 - 1$.

the exp1 of Expon1

where *Expon1* is a local variable.

NOTE

Using the Exp1 function with a number is the same as entering

the exp of <number> — 1

SEE ALSO

Exp function
Exp2 function

Exp2

Returns the base-2 exponent of the value specified as the *<number>* argument.

FORMS

exp2(<number>)

the exp2 of <number>

ARGUMENT

<number>   Refers to a value or an expression that results in a value. It can also refer to a HyperCard container that holds such a value or expression.

USAGE

Using the Exp2 function is the same as raising 2 by the power of that number. Therefore, the two expressions

exp2(6)
2 ^ 6

yield the same result: 64.

EXAMPLES

the exp2 of 16

which is the same as 2^{16}.

exp2(newVal)

where *newVal* is a variable that contains a value.

SEE ALSO

Exp function
Exp1 function

Length

Returns the number of characters in the $<source>$ specified as the function argument.

FORMS

    the length of $<$**source**$>$

    length($<$**source**$>$**)**

ARGUMENT

    $<source>$ Refers to a text string (enclosed in quotation marks) entered as the argument or to any HyperCard container that holds such a character string. The $<source>$ argument can also refer to just a part of a string held in such a container specified by a chunk expression (see Chunking Expressions in the section on HyperCard Containers in Chapter 1).

USAGE

The Length function is used to return the total number of characters in a particular HyperCard container. When calculating the number of characters, the return characters in the container are included as part of the count. Often, you will use an If...Then construction with the Length function to determine the action that the script is to take as a result of the number of characters in a particular field or variable.

EXAMPLES

   the length of line 2 of field "Address"

   length(second word of last item of field 4)

   the length of temp

where *temp* is a variable that contains a string of text.

Ln

Returns the natural logarithm—that is, the logarithm in base *e*—of the number specified.

FORMS

ln(<number>)

the ln of <number>

ARGUMENT

<number>   Refers to a value or an expression that results in a value. It can also refer to a HyperCard container that holds such a value or expression. Note that the value specified for the *<number>* argument must be greater than zero.

USAGE

The Ln function is used to calculate the base-*e* (where the constant *e* is equal to 2.7182818) logarithm of a value.

EXAMPLES

ln(10)

ln(logNumber)

where *logNumber* is a local variable that holds a number.

Ln1

Returns the natural logarithm of 1 plus the number specified.

FORMS

ln1(<number>)
the ln1 of <number>

ARGUMENT

<number>   Refers to a value or an expression that results in a value. It can also refer to a HyperCard container that holds such a value or expression.

USAGE

The Ln1 function is used to calculate the base-*e* (where the constant *e* is equal to 2.7182818) logarithm plus 1 of a value, or

$$\ln (n) + 1$$

where *n* is the value.

EXAMPLES

ln1(9)

which could also be written as ln(9) + 1.

the ln1 of logNumber1

where *logNumber1* is a local variable that holds a value.

Log2

Returns the base-2 log of the number specified.

log2(<number>)
the log2 of <**number**>

   <number>   Refers to a value or an expression that results in a value. It can also refer to a HyperCard container that holds such a value or expression.

The Log2 function is used to calculate the logarithm in base 2 for the *<number>* specified as the argument.

   log2(78)

returns 6.285402.

   log2(logNumber)

where *logNumber* is a local variable.

Max

Returns the highest number in the list of numbers specified.

FORM

max(<number list>)

ARGUMENT

<*number list*> Refers to a list of values or expressions that return values entered as the argument, or to a list of HyperCard containers that hold such values or expressions. Each number or container name in the list must be separated by commas, and the entire number list must be enclosed in parentheses.

USAGE

The Max function is used to return the highest value among those specified in the <*number list*> argument. Even if you enter the names of HyperCard containers in the <*number list*> argument, the program still returns the number from the container that holds the highest value, rather than the name of the container.

EXAMPLES

max(5*4, 16, 300/12)

returns 25, which is equal to 300/12.

put max(field 1, field 2, field 3) into msg

In this example, HyperCard evaluates the values in the first three fields of the current card. If field 2 holds the highest value, 1050, then the Max function puts this number in the Message box.

SEE ALSO

Min function

Min

Returns the lowest number in the list of numbers specified.

FORM

min(<number list>)

ARGUMENT

<*number*
list>

Refers to a list of values or expressions that return values entered as the argument, or to a list of HyperCard containers that hold such values or expressions. Each number or container name in the list must be separated by commas, and the entire number list must be enclosed in parentheses.

USAGE

The Min function is used to return the lowest value among those specified in the <*number list*> argument. Even if you enter the names of HyperCard containers in the <*number list*> argument, the program still returns the number from the container that holds the lowest value, rather than the name of the container.

EXAMPLES

min(16, 23, 40*.66)

returns 16, the lowest value.

put min(field 5, field 10, field 7) into field 11

In this example, HyperCard evaluates the values in field 5, field 7, and field 10 of the current card. If field 10 holds the lowest value, 0.125, then the Max function puts this number in field 11 of the card.

SEE ALSO

Max function

Mouse

Tells you whether the mouse button is down or up.

FORM

the mouse

ARGUMENTS

The Mouse function does not require any arguments.

USAGE

The Mouse function returns *down* if the mouse button is being pressed at the time the message handler containing the function is executed. It returns *up* if the mouse button is not being pressed. The Mouse function is often used in If...Then constructions to determine the next action to be taken by the script according to whether the mouse button is down or up.

EXAMPLES

wait until the mouse is down

causes the script to pause until the mouse button is pressed.

if the mouse is down then show message box

MouseClick

Tells you whether the mouse button has been clicked.

FORM

the mouseClick

ARGUMENTS

The MouseClick function does not require any arguments.

USAGE

The MouseClick function returns *true* if the mouse has been clicked since the message began. It returns *false* if the mouse has not been clicked. This function is often used in Repeat constructions to determine how long the loop is to be repeated. It can also be used with one of the forms of the Wait command to determine when the execution of the script is to be continued.

EXAMPLES

wait until the mouseClick

causes the script to pause until the next click of the mouse button.

repeat until the mouseClick
   .
   .
   .
end repeat

MouseH

Returns the horizontal screen coordinate of the cursor.

FORM

the mouseH

ARGUMENTS

The MouseH function does not require any arguments.

USAGE

The MouseH function returns just the horizontal screen coordinate of the cursor position when the message handler that contains this function is executed. The horizontal coordinates of the HyperCard screen range from 0 to 512. The coordinate number returned by the function represents the number of pixels counted across the screen from the upper left corner of the screen, which has a horizontal coordinate number of 0.

EXAMPLE

if the mouseH > 250 then show tool window at 15,100

NOTE

The MouseH function must be prefaced by the word *the* in the script.

SEE ALSO

MouseLoc function
MouseV function

MouseLoc

Returns the horizontal and vertical screen coordinates of the cursor.

FORM

the mouseLoc

ARGUMENTS

The MouseLoc function does not require any arguments.

USAGE

The MouseLoc function returns both the horizontal and vertical screen coordinates of the cursor position when the message handler that contains this function is executed. The horizontal coordinate number is listed before the vertical coordinate number, and they are separated by a comma. The coordinate numbers returned by the function represent the number of pixels counted across and down from the upper left corner of the screen, which has the coordinate numbers 0,0.

EXAMPLES

get the mouseLoc

This command is useful for obtaining the position of the cursor.

show the tool window at the mouseLoc

This command instructs the program to place the Tools menu with its upper left corner at the cursor position.

NOTE ════════════

The MouseLoc function must be prefaced by the word *the* in the script.

SEE ALSO ════════════

MouseH function
MouseV function

MouseV

Returns the vertical screen coordinate of the cursor.

FORM

the mouseV

ARGUMENTS

The MouseV function does not require any arguments.

USAGE

The MouseV function returns just the vertical screen coordinate of the cursor position when the message handler that contains this function is executed. The vertical coordinates of the HyperCard screen range from 0 to 342. The coordinate number returned by the function represents the number of pixels counted down from the upper left corner of the screen, which has a vertical coordinate number of 0.

EXAMPLE

if the mouseV > = 200 then hide message box

This command creates extra space on the screen, if the cursor is between vertical coordinates 200 and 342, by hiding the Message box.

NOTE

The MouseV function must be prefaced by the word *the* in the script.

SEE ALSO

MouseH function
MouseLoc function

Number

Returns the number of cards, buttons, or fields in the stack. Also returns the number of components that there are in a HyperCard container.

FORMS

[the] **number of cards** | **buttons** | **fields**

[the] **number of** <**components**> **in** <**container**>

ARGUMENTS

[the]	Optional in both forms of the function
cards | *buttons* | *fields*	Refers to the object in the stack that is current when the function is executed.
<*components*>	Refers to the name of the text component—such as the chars, items, words, and lines—as given by a chunk expression.
<*container*>	Refers to the name of the HyperCard container that holds the text components (or chunks) whose number is to be calculated.

USAGE

The Number function can be used to determine the number of objects in the current stack, such as the number of cards, fields, or buttons. When using this function to find out the number of card fields in a stack (as opposed to background fields), you need to add *card* to the *fields* argument. When using this function to find out the number of background buttons in a stack (as opposed to card buttons), you need to add *bkgnd* to the *buttons* argument.

The Number function can also be used to calculate the number of text components, such as the number of characters, items, words, or lines, in a particular HyperCard container such as a field or variable. When entering a chunk expression as the <*components*> argument, be sure that it is ordered from the smallest to largest chunk in the <*container*> (see the last example in the following section).

EXAMPLES =========================

the number of cards

gives you the number of cards in the current stack.

the number of buttons

gives you the number of card buttons in the current stack.

number of card fields

number of lines of field "Address"

the number of items in field 3

number of chars in word 2 of line 4 of card field 1

NumToChar

Returns the character equivalent of the ASCII decimal code number specified as the function argument.

FORMS

numToChar(<number>)

the numToChar of <number>

ARGUMENT

<number>   Refers to the ASCII decimal code value or an expression that results in a value. It can also refer to a HyperCard container that holds such a value or expression.

USAGE

The NumToChar function is used to return the ASCII character that is equivalent to a particular number given as the function argument. This function is the complement of the CharToNum function, which returns the ASCII code number equivalent for a particular keyboard character.

EXAMPLES

numToChar(65) -- returns A

the numToChar of 97 -- returns a

NOTE

Some characters returned by the NumToChar function cannot be seen on the screen. For example, entering

numToChar(32)

returns a space, even though you cannot see it on the screen.

SEE ALSO

CharToNum function

Offset

Returns the starting position of a substring (the <*text1*> argument) within another text string (the <*text2*> argument).

FORM

offset(<text1>,<text2>)

ARGUMENTS

<*text1*> and <*text2*>   Refer to character strings enclosed in quotation marks or HyperCard containers that hold such strings. The <*text1*> argument refers specifically to the substring whose starting position is to be located within the string in the <*text2*> argument. If the <*text1*> string is not found within the <*text2*> string, the function returns 0 as the result.

USAGE

The Offset function lets you locate the starting position of a particular portion of text (often referred to as the *substring*) that is contained within other text (referred to as the *string*). The number returned by the function represents the number of the character where the substring begins. The Offset function can be used to locate the starting position of any characters within a text string. However, it can only locate the position of the first occurrence of duplicate characters in the same string.

EXAMPLES

If field 3 contains the text string *San Francisco, CA* and you enter

put offset("San",field 3)into startPos

the memory variable startPos will contain 1 because *San* begins at the first position in the text string *San Francisco, CA.*
    If you enter

put offset("Fran",field 3)into startPos

the startPos variable will contain 5 because the text string *Fran* begins at the fifth position in field 3.
    If you enter

put offset("o",field 3)into startPos

the variable will contain 13 because the *o* in *Francisco* occurs in the thirteenth position in field 3.

OptionKey

Tells you whether the Option key is up or down.

FORM

the optionKey

ARGUMENT

The OptionKey function does not require any arguments.

USAGE

The OptionKey function returns *down* if the Option key is depressed when the message handler containing this function is executed, or it returns *up* if it is not depressed. It can be used with If...Then constructions to determine the next action of the script depending on whether this special key has been used.

EXAMPLE

if the optionKey is down then
    choose rectangle tool
end if

SEE ALSO

CommandKey
ShiftKey

Param

Returns a single parameter of the most recently sent message when you specify the position of the parameter.

FORMS

the param of <number>

param(<number>)

ARGUMENT

<number>   Refers to a value or an expression that results
              in a value. It can also refer to a HyperCard
              container that holds such a value or expres-
              sion. Enter 0 as the <number> argument to
              get the command word itself. Enter 1 as the
              argument to get the first word after the com-
              mand word, and so on.

USAGE

The Param function is used to return a single parameter from a list of parameters in the current message. To use it, you must know the position of the parameter you wish to extract. HyperTalk considers the message name to be position 0 and each parameter that follows the message name to increase by a count of 1. For example, to get the first argument of a message handler, you would enter

the param of 1

into the script. You can use the Param function to pass a particular argument to a new message handler (see Message Handlers in Chapter 1).

EXAMPLES

if param(1) is empty then go Home

put the param of 0 into paramMsg

where *paramMsg* is a variable.

SEE ALSO

ParamCount function
Params function

ParamCount

Returns the total number of parameters in the current message.

FORM

the paramCount

ARGUMENTS

The ParamCount function does not require any arguments.

USAGE

The ParamCount function is used to get the total number of parameters in the currently executed message. Unlike the Param or Params function, both of which return the text of the message, the ParamCount function returns only a value representing the number of parameters of the message. This number includes the name of the message as part of this calculated value. The ParamCount function is often used as part of Repeat constructions where a counter loop is to be set up that repeats the loop up to the number of parameters in the current message (see HyperTalk Control Structures in Chapter 1).

EXAMPLES

if the paramCount is 0 then go to stack "Stack Help"

put the paramCount into paramNumber

where *paramNumber* is a variable.

SEE ALSO

Param function
Params function

Params

Returns the entire current message along with the command word.

FORM

the params

ARGUMENTS

The Params function does not require any arguments.

USAGE

The Params function is used to return the entire text of the current message. When used with the Get command, as in *get params*, the current message including the name of the message and all parameters specified are placed in the *it* variable. From there, you can use the appropriate chunk expression to pass just a part of the message to other scripts.

EXAMPLES

if the params is "mouseUp" then go to stack "Info"

where MouseUp is the name of the current message.

get the params

Used with the Get command, the program puts the entire text of the current message (including the message name) into the *it* variable.

SEE ALSO

Param function
ParamCount function

Random

Returns a random number between 1 and the number specified. The <*number*> specified in the argument is used as the upper limit of the Random function.

random(<number>)

the random of <number>

<*number*>　　　Refers to a value or an expression that results in a value. It can also refer to a HyperCard container that holds such a value or expression. The number can be any integer up to 32767.

The Random function allows you to add a random number to the scripts that you write. The Random function will return a number between 1 and the upward limit specified as the <*number*> argument. You can effectively use the Random function as the argument of various HyperCard commands in stacks that call for varied screen displays each time it is used.

EXAMPLES

random(5) – – returns a number between 1 and 5

the random of highNumber

where *highNumber* is a variable.

Result

Holds the text of an error message explaining what went wrong in the previous command. Normally, *the result* is empty.

FORM

the result

ARGUMENTS

The Result function does not require any arguments.

USAGE

The Result function is used to return the last error message generated by the Go or Find HyperTalk command when either of them fails to locate the card or search string specified by the user. *The result* is empty when no error is generated. Therefore, you can use the Result function with the Ask command to have the program display an error message of your own (see the example in the following section).

EXAMPLE

```
find "George" in field 1
if the result < > empty then
    ask "You have not yet made an entry for George"
end if
```

Round

Rounds the number specified up or down to the nearest whole number.

FORMS

round(<number>)
the round of <number>

ARGUMENT

<number>   Refers to a value or an expression that results in a value. It can also refer to a HyperCard container that holds such a value or expression.

USAGE

The Round function gives you the ability to change the precision of a fractional number that is calculated by the program or stored in a particular HyperCard container to the nearest integer. If the fraction of the number is .5 or less, the number is rounded down to the nearest whole number. If it is greater than .5, the number is rounded up to the nearest whole number.

EXAMPLES

round(4.5) -- returns 4
round(4.51) -- returns 5

SEE ALSO

Trunc function

Seconds

Returns the number of seconds since the first second of the year 1904 (0:00:00 hour on January 1, 1904), the reference point used in HyperCard date and time calculations.

FORMS

the seconds

the secs

ARGUMENTS

The Seconds function does not require any arguments.

USAGE

The Seconds function is used in elapsed time calculations. This function calculates the number of seconds between the moment it is executed and the standard Macintosh reference point (the first second of 1904). Thus, by using it at different times in the script, you can have the program calculate and report on the elapsed time between various events (see the example in the following section).

EXAMPLE

```
on mouseUp
   ask "Enter number of cards to print:" with 1
   put the seconds into startPrint
   open printing
   print it cards
```

```
  close printing
  put "Elapsed printing time is" ¬
  && the seconds − startPrint && "seconds." ¬
  into the message box
end mouseUp
```

This script calculates the elapsed printing time.

SEE ALSO

Ticks function

ShiftKey

Tells you whether the Shift key is depressed.

FORM

the shiftKey

ARGUMENTS

The ShiftKey function does not require any arguments.

USAGE

The ShiftKey function returns *down* if the Shift key is depressed when the message handler that contains it is executed. It returns *up* if this key is not depressed. It can be used with If...Then constructions to determine the next action of the script, depending on whether this key has been used.

EXAMPLE

**if the shiftKey is down then
  hide the message box
end if**

SEE ALSO

CommandKey function
OptionKey function

Sin

Returns the sine of the angle specified in radians.

FORMS

sin(<angle in radians>)

the sin of <angle in radians>

ARGUMENT

<angle in radians>   Refers to the number of radians or to an expression that yields this number. This value or expression can be entered directly as the argument or indirectly by entering the name of the HyperCard container that holds such a value or expression.

USAGE

The Sin function is used to calculate the sine of an angle expressed in radians. To convert an angle expressed in degrees to radians for use with this function, multiply the number by Pi (the constant that holds the value of π to 20 places) and then divide it by 180 (see the first example in the Examples section).

EXAMPLES

sin(45 * pi/180)

where *pi/180* converts the 45° angle to radians.

sin(acuteAngle)

where *acuteAngle* is a local variable.

SEE ALSO

Atan function
Cos function
Tan function
Pi constant: Chapter 5

Sound

Returns the name of the voice that is playing, or *done* if no sound is being produced with the Play command.

FORM

the sound

ARGUMENTS

The Sound function does not require any arguments.

USAGE

The Sound function works much like the Result function. It reports on whether any sound is being produced by the Play command. If no sound is produced, the result is empty. If a sound is being produced, it returns the name of its voice. You can use it in scripts that produce sounds with the Play command to tell you whether the Play command is finished. If it is finished, you can then have the program go on and perform a new action.

EXAMPLE

if the sound is "done" then
go to stack "New Music"
end if

SEE ALSO

Play command: Chapter 2

Sqrt

Returns the square root of the number specified as the function argument.

FORMS

sqrt(<number>)
the sqrt of <number>

ARGUMENT

<number>   Refers to a value or to an expression that results in a value. It can also refer to a HyperCard container that holds such a value or expression.

USAGE

The Sqrt function is a mathematical expression that calculates the square root of the value or expression entered as the *<number>* argument. The *<number>* argument can contain other nested mathematical functions as well as simple arithmetic calculations (see the second example in the following section).

EXAMPLES

sqrt(45*7 − 2.5)

computes the square root of $45*7-2.5$, or 312.5, which is 17.68.

sqrt(sin(45))

computes the square root of the sin of an angle measuring 45 radians.

sqrt(temp)

where *temp* is a variable.

Tan

Returns the tangent of the angle specified in radians.

tan(<angle in radians>)

the tan of <angle in radians>

<angle in radians>

Refers to the number of radians or to an expression that yields this number. This value or expression can be entered directly as the argument or indirectly by entering the name of the HyperCard container that holds such a value or expression.

The Tan function is used to calculate the tangent of an angle expressed in radians. To convert an angle expressed in degrees to radians for use with this function, multiply the number by Pi (the constant that holds the value of π to 20 places) and then divide it by 180 (see the first example in the Examples section).

tan(32.5 * pi/180)

where *pi/180* converts the 32.5° angle to radians.

tan(angleB)

where *angleB* is a variable.

SEE ALSO

Atan function
Cos function
Sin function
Pi constant: Chapter 5

Target

Returns the ID number of the original object that received the current message.

the target

The Target function does not require any arguments.

The Target function identifies the HyperCard object that is the original recipient of the message currently being sent or last sent by the program. When used, it returns a string that contains the ID number or name of this object. For example, if you use the Next button from the Home Card and then enter *the target* in the Message box, HyperCard will return

card "Stacks"

as the recipient of the *go to next card* message in the Next button script.

The Target function can be used to obtain the name of the object or to pass a new message to that object (with the Send command; see the first example in the Examples section). It can also be used in button scripts to supply the short name of the target object as the argument of a particular HyperTalk command (see the third example in the following section).

```
send mouseUp to the target
get the name of the target

on mouseUp
  get short name of the target
  open it
end mouseUp
```

This example shows the background script, which uses the Target function to supply the name of the application button clicked on last as the argument of the Open command.

```
put the target into targetID
```

where *targetID* is a variable.

Ticks

Returns the number of ticks (each tick is equal to 1/60th of a second) since the Macintosh was started up or rebooted.

FORM

the ticks

ARGUMENTS

The Ticks function does not require any arguments.

USAGE

The Ticks function is similar to the Seconds function except that it returns the number of ticks (with each tick equivalent to 1/60th of a second) since the Macintosh was turned on or last restarted. Like the Seconds function, the Ticks function can also be used to calculate and report on the elapsed time between one action and another in the script (see the example in the following section). To convert the number of ticks returned by this function into seconds, divide the result by 60.

EXAMPLE

```
on mouseUp
  put the ticks into tickNumber
  show all cards
  put (the ticks − tickNumber)/60 && ¬
  "seconds have elapsed" into the message box
end mouseUp
```

This script calculates the elapsed time in seconds.

SEE ALSO

Seconds function

Time

Returns the current time from the Macintosh internal clock.

FORMS

the time – – 10:49 AM

the short time – – 10:49 AM

the long time – – 10:49:52 AM

ARGUMENTS

The Time function does not require any arguments.

USAGE

The Time function returns the current time as kept by the Macintosh internal clock. You can get the (short) time or the long time (the long time includes seconds). If the Time option on the Control Panel is set for a 12-hour clock, the time string returned by the function will be terminated by either AM or PM. Otherwise, the time string returned by the function will be given according to a 24-hour clock.

When using *the time* (or *the short time*) or *the long time* in a calculation, convert the result of the Time function into seconds using the Convert command (see Convert in Chapter 2 for more information).

EXAMPLES

put the long time into field 2

put the time into now – – now is local memory variable
convert now to seconds

```
convert field 1 to seconds
subtract field 1 from now
convert now to short time
put now into field 3
```

Since this script involves a calculation, all values to be calculated are first converted to seconds.

SEE ALSO

Date function
Convert command: Chapter 2

Tool

Returns the name of the tool currently chosen.

FORM

the tool

ARGUMENTS

The Tool function does not require any arguments.

USAGE

The Tool function returns the name of tool that is currently selected from the Tools menu. The tool names are as follows:

browse tool	spray tool
button tool	rectangle tool
field tool	round rect tool
select tool	bucket tool
lasso tool	oval tool
pencil tool	curve tool
brush tool	text tool
eraser tool	regular polygon tool
line tool	polygon tool

EXAMPLE

if the tool < > "browse tool" then
   choose "browse tool"
   .
   .
   .
end if

The Tool function is most often used with the Choose command in a script to ensure that the proper tool is selected before new actions using the tool are executed.

SEE ALSO

Choose command: Chapter 2

Trunc

Drops the fractional part of any decimal number specified as the function argument and returns the whole number.

FORMS

trunc(<number>)

the trunc of <number>

ARGUMENT

<number>   Refers to a value or an expression that results in a value. It can also refer to a HyperCard container that holds such a value or expression.

USAGE

The Trunc function is used to drop the fraction (that is, all values to the right of the decimal point) from a number. Unlike the Round function, the Trunc function has no effect on the integer portion of the number. You can use this function in any script where you need only the integer portion of the number that is entered in a container or calculated by an expression.

EXAMPLES

trunc(56.345) – – returns 56

the trunc of 0.456 – – returns 0

SEE ALSO

Round function

Value

Converts a string of text into an expression that can be evaluated.

FORMS

value(<expression>)

the value of <expression>

ARGUMENT

<expression>   Refers to any HyperCard container that holds a mathematical expression entered as a text string (enclosed in quotation marks in the case of variables and the Message box).

USAGE

The Value function enables you to convert expressions stored as text strings in HyperCard containers into mathematical expressions that are calculated. It can also be used, in a very limited way, to perform calculations between numbers entered by name rather than by digit into containers such as a text field or variable. Note, however, that HyperCard can only understand the names of whole numbers between 0 and 10 (as in zero, one, two, and so on). Also, you must use the mathematical symbols for addition (+), subtraction (−), multiplication (*), and division (/) operators used in the expression, as HyperCard does not understand the use of English words such as *plus*, *minus*, *times*, and *divided by*.

EXAMPLES

If the first line of field 5 in the card contains the text 4 + (10 * 2) and you enter the command

put the value of card field 5 into field 7

then field 7 will contain 24.

If you enter the statement

the value of three * four

in the Message box, the program will return 12 as the result.

CHAPTER 4

Properties in HyperTalk

All HyperCard objects have characteristics called *properties* that you can retrieve and set from the scripts you write. When operating HyperCard from the menus, you can reset most of these properties by clicking on new settings that appear in related dialog boxes. In HyperTalk scripts, you retrieve information about the current settings with the Get or Put command and make changes to the settings with the Set command (see Chapter 2 for specific information on the use of these commands).

Not all HyperCard properties can be changed with the Set command, however. For example, although you can use the Get command to retrieve the ID number assigned to an object such as a field or button, you cannot change this number with the Set command. Those properties that cannot be reset are clearly indicated in this chapter. Also, when using the Get and Set commands with the HyperCard properties, the word *the* before the property name is always optional.

HyperCard properties are divided into eight hierarchical categories, starting from the most comprehensive level: global, paint, window, stack, background, card, field, and button properties (see Table 4.1). In this chapter, the properties are listed alphabetically within these classifications. However, because the background and card properties are the same, you will find their properties listed under one heading. Note that the Text... properties for paint text, field, and button properties are described in the Paint Properties section.

PROPERTIES	GLOBAL	PAINT	WINDOW	STACK	BKGND	CARD	FIELD	BUTTON
AutoHilite								■
BlindTyping	■							
Brush		■						
Centered		■						
Cursor	■							
DragSpeed	■							
EditBkgnd	■							
Filled		■						
FreeSize				■				
Grid		■						
Hilite								■
Icon							■	■
ID					■	■	■	■
LineSize		■						
Loc(ation)			■			■	■	■
LockMessages	■							
LockRecent	■							
LockScreen	■							
LockText							■	
Multiple		■						
MultiSpace		■						
Name				■	■	■	■	■
Number				■	■	■	■	■
NumberFormat	■							
Pattern		■						
PolySides		■						
PowerKeys	■							
Rect(angle)			■				■	■
Script				■	■	■	■	■
Scroll			■				■	

Table 4.1: HyperCard Properties

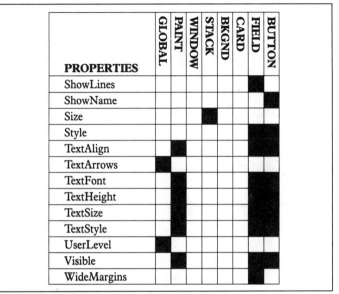

PROPERTIES	GLOBAL	PAINT	WINDOW	STACK	BKGND	CARD	FIELD	BUTTON
ShowLines							■	
ShowName							■	■
Size				■				
Style							■	■
TextAlign		■					■	■
TextArrows	■							
TextFont		■					■	■
TextHeight		■					■	
TextSize		■					■	■
TextStyle		■					■	■
UserLevel	■							
Visible		■					■	■
WideMargins							■	

Table 4.1: HyperCard Properties (continued)

GLOBAL PROPERTIES

Global properties are those that apply to all stacks in HyperCard. They can be thought of as the properties of HyperCard itself.

BlindTyping

Allows you to type HyperTalk commands into the Message box even when it is hidden, when BlindTyping is set to true.

USAGE

The BlindTyping property is used to set the ability to type Hyper-Talk commands into the Message box even when it is not visible on the screen. It can also be used with the Get command to return the current status of blind typing. Setting the BlindTyping property to true is the same as checking the BlindTyping box on the User Preferences card in the Home stack. Setting the BlindTyping property to false is the same as unchecking the BlindTyping box on this card.

When blind typing is in effect and you type a HyperTalk command, you are literally typing blind. If you make a typing mistake, you will not be able to see it on the screen. When you press Return, the program will attempt to interpret the command as entered. If the command contains typing errors, you will have to reenter it from scratch. You will not be able to edit, as you can when the Message box is visible on the screen.

EXAMPLES

get blindTyping

set the blindTyping to true

Cursor

Controls the shape of the cursor during the execution of a script.

USAGE

There are four cursor shapes that you can set by entering their ID numbers: 1 produces the I-Beam cursor, 2 the standard crossbar, 3 a thick version of the crossbar, and 4 the wristwatch icon (typically denoting that HyperCard is busy and you must wait).

The cursor returns to its normal shape as soon as the script ends. You cannot use the Get command with the Cursor property. You can only change the cursor shape with the Set command.

EXAMPLES

```
set the cursor to 1  – –  I-Beam cursor
set cursor to 2  – –  standard crossbar cursor
set cursor to 3  – –  thick version of crossbar cursor
set the cursor to 4  – –  wristwatch cursor
```

DragSpeed

Controls the speed at which the Drag command operates.

USAGE

The DragSpeed property can be used to set a new speed that the cursor travels when the Drag command is used. When setting a new drag speed, you enter a number as the part of the Set command argument that represents the pixels per second. Setting the DragSpeed property to 0 produces the fastest speed on the Macintosh. To watch drawing on the screen, set the speed to 150.

EXAMPLES

get the dragSpeed
set dragSpeed to 75
set the dragSpeed to 170

EditBkgnd

Takes you from the background of a stack to the card level and vice versa.

USAGE

Setting the EditBkgnd property to true is the same as selecting the Background option on the Edit menu when you are at the card level. Setting the EditBkgnd property to false is the same as selecting the Background option when you are in the background.

You can use this property to ensure that you are at the correct level (either the background or card level) before executing HyperTalk commands in the script that make editing changes to the card.

EXAMPLES

get editBkgnd

set the editBkgnd to false

set the editBkgnd to true

LockMessages

Stops system messages from being sent by HyperCard.

USAGE

When the LockMessages property is set to true, all of the system messages—MouseUp, OpenCard, and so on—are not sent up the HyperCard message hierarchy. This can be used to speed up the processing of scripts that do not depend upon receiving system messages. However, it cannot be used in most scripts where this is not the case. If you do use the Set commmand to set the LockMessages property to true, be sure that you add a corresponding Set command that sets the LockMessages property to false right before the end of the script.

EXAMPLES

    get the lockMessages

    set the lockMessages to true

    set lockMessages to false

LockRecent

Controls whether the program adds miniature cards to the Recent card.

Normally, HyperCard adds a miniature version of each unique card
that is visited in a stack. When you set the LockRecent property to
true with the Set command, this procedure is not followed. You can
use this wherever you do not want the user to be able to revisit the
card by selecting the Recent option from the Go menu. When
the LockRecent property is set to false, miniatures of the last 42
unique cards are added to the Recent card.

EXAMPLES

get the lockRecent

set lockRecent to true

set the lockRecent to false

LockScreen

Determines whether the screen display is updated during the execution of a series of HyperTalk commands.

USAGE

When the LockScreen property is set to true, HyperCard freezes the screen display during the execution of the HyperTalk commands that follow the Set command in the script. When the LockScreen property is set to false, the user sees all updates on the screen as the program executes the HyperTalk commands that follow the Set command in the script.

For every Set command in a script that sets the LockScreen property to true, there should be a corresponding Set command that sets the LockScreen property to false after the commands that are to be executed behind the scenes.

EXAMPLES

get lockScreen

set the lockScreen to true

set the lockScreen to false

NumberFormat

Sets the display format for all numerical results calculated by Hyper-Talk's math operators and commands.

USAGE

The NumberFormat property is used to format the display of deci-mal places throughout HyperCard. When a new number format is set, all calculated numbers entered from then on are displayed according the format string used. This format string is entered as part of the argument of the Set command enclosed in quotation marks. Enter zero (0) in the format string for any decimal place that is always required even when the place value is zero. Enter the num-ber symbol (#) for any decimal place that is required only when the place value is not zero. The number of zeros and/or number symbols entered after the decimal point determines the precision of the numerical display.

Note that when a new number format is set, it affects only num-bers that are added or recalculated after that time. Once values are entered into fields, they are held as text strings that are not affected by the number format in effect.

Also, although NumberFormat is a global property that affects all numerical entries and calculations, the program automatically resets the format to the default setting whenever an Idle system mes-sage is sent. This means that you must set the number format as part of a script of an object and that you cannot change it from the Message box. The default number format string used by HyperCard is 0.######.

EXAMPLES

get the numberFormat

set numberFormat to "0.00"

set the numberFormat to "00.###"

PowerKeys

Determines whether the power keys used in the painting program are active.

USAGE

When you set the PowerKeys property to true, the power keys for the HyperCard painting program are activated. Power keys enable the user to select most of the painting program options by typing a single letter from the keyboard (see Table 4.2). When you set the PowerKeys property to false, the power keys are deactivated. The power keys can also be turned on and off by checking or unchecking the Power Keys box on the User Preferences card in the Home stack.

EXAMPLES

get the powerKeys

set the powerKeys to true

set powerKeys to false

	KEY	COMMAND
Paint menu	A	Select All (Command-A)
	D	Darken
	E	Trace Edges
	F	Fill
	H	Flip Horizontal
	I	Invert
	L	Lighten
	O	Opaque
	P	Pickup
	R	Revert
	S	Select (Command-S)
	T	Transparent
	V	Flip Vertical
	[	Rotate Left
	]	Rotate Right
Options menu	C	Draw Centered (on/off)
	G	Grid (on/off)
	M	Draw Multiple (on/off)
	1, 2, 3, 4, 6, 8	Line Size (number of pixels)
Patterns menu	B	Black pattern
	W	White pattern

Table 4.2: The Power Keys for the Painting Program

TextArrows

Controls whether the arrow keys move the user from card to card or move the cursor in a field.

USAGE

When the TextArrows property is set to true, the arrow keys can be used to move the cursor within text fields and the Message box. When the TextArrows property is set to false, the arrow keys move the user to new cards in the stack. Once the TextArrows property is set to true, the user can navigate through the cards in the stack by pressing the Option key and an arrow key.

Resetting this property in a script is the same as checking or unchecking the Text Arrows box in the User Preferences card in the Home stack.

EXAMPLES

get the textArrows

set textArrows to true

set the textArrows to false

NOTE

The TextArrows property was added to version 1.1 of HyperCard. You will not be able to use this property if you are still using an earlier version of this program (see your Macintosh dealer for an update to version 1.1).

UserLevel

Sets the user level from a script.

The user level determines what HyperCard menu options are available to the user. You can change the user level by using the Set command with the UserLevel property followed by a number between 1 and 5. The user levels and their numerical equivalents are as follows:

User Level	Number
Browsing	1
Typing	2
Painting	3
Authoring	4
Scripting	5

```
get userLevel
if it > 2 then
   set userLevel to 2
end if
```

PAINT PROPERTIES

The paint properties allow you to control many of the painting program attributes from the scripts you write. These include the shape of tools such as the Brush and Line tools; the current pattern; drawing attributes such as centered, multiple, and multispace; and paint text attributes such as font, text size, and text height.

Brush

Determines the brush shape used by the Brush tool.

USAGE

There are 32 different brush shapes that can be used by the Brush tool in drawing. Figure 4.1 shows you the dialog box that contains these shapes. When you assign a new brush shape from a HyperTalk script, you use the Brush property with the Set command followed by a number between 1 and 32. The brush shapes in the dialog box in Figure 4.1 are numbered from 1 for the brush shape in the upper left corner of the dialog box and increasing down the first column and across subsequent columns (therefore, the brush shape number for the last shape in the first column is 4, and that of the last shape in the last column—in the lower right corner—is 32). When you use the Brush property with the Set command to assign a new brush shape, this is the same as clicking on the appropriate brush shape in this dialog box.

get the brush
set the brush to 5
set brush to 10

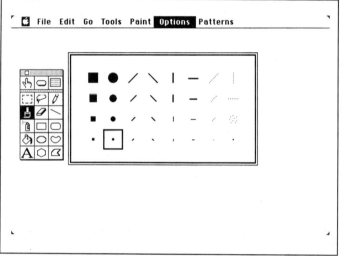

Figure 4.1: The Brush Shape selection box

Centered

Turns the Draw Centered option on and off.

USAGE

When the Centered property is set to true, the Draw Centered option on the Options menu is turned on. With the Draw Centered option on, figures created with tools such as the Line, Rectangle, Oval, and so on, are drawn from the center outward instead of from one side. When the Centered property is set to false, the Draw Centered option is turned off.

EXAMPLES

get the centered

set centered to true

set the centered to false

Filled

Turns the Draw Filled option on and off.

When the Filled property is set to true, the Draw Filled option on the Options menu is turned on. With the Draw Filled option on, the currently selected pattern is used to fill figures as you draw them. When the Filled property is set to false, the Draw Filled option is turned off.

get the filled

set the filled to true

set filled to false

Grid

Turns the painting grid on and off.

USAGE

When the Grid property is set to true, the painting grid is turned
on. With the Grid option on, drawing with various paint tools is
constricted to an invisible grid eight pixels square. Each horizontal
(and vertical) line is eight pixels apart. When the Grid property is
set to false, the painting grid is turned off.

EXAMPLES
---

get the grid

set the grid to true

set the grid to false

LineSize

Sets the thickness of the line size used by various painting tools.

The LineSize property can be used to describe or reset the thickness
of the line drawn by painting tools such as the Line, Rectangle,
Oval, and so on. The line size is changed by using the Set command
with this property followed by the number of pixels for the line size.
You can set the pixel width to 1, 2, 3, 4, 6, or 8 pixels. Using this
property with the Set command is the same as selecting a new line
size from the Line Size selection box (shown in Figure 4.2) on the
Options menu of the painting program.

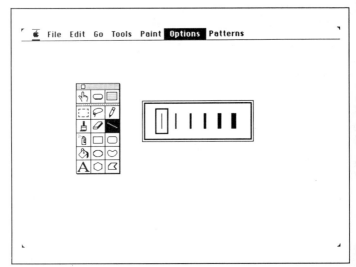

Figure 4.2: The Line Size selection box

EXAMPLES

get the lineSize
set the lineSize to 2
set lineSize to 4

Multiple

Turns on and off the Draw Multiple option on the Options menu.

USAGE

When the Multiple property is set to true, the Draw Multiple option is activated. With the Draw Multiple option on, the program draws multiple images with the selected Paint tool as the user (or script) drags the mouse across the screen. The spacing of these images can be controlled with the MultiSpace property. When the Multiple property is set to false, the Draw Multiple option is deactivated.

EXAMPLES

get the multiple

set the multiple to true

set multiple to false

SEE ALSO

MultiSpace (paint) property
Drag command: Chapter 2

MultiSpace

Sets the spacing between multiple images when the Draw Multiple option is active.

USAGE

The MultiSpace property can be used to control the amount of spacing (density) of multiple copies of a figure drawn with the Draw Multiple option on. To set a new spacing, you use the Set command with the property followed by a number from 1 to 9. The lower the number, the denser the spacing of the multiple images that are drawn. Figure 4.3 shows you an example with multiple images of a triangle drawn using various spacing settings.

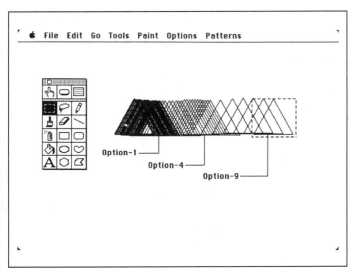

Figure 4.3: Multiple copies of an image with varied spacing

set the multiSpace to 1
set multiSpace to 4
set the multiSpace to 9

Multiple (paint) property

Pattern

Sets the current pattern selected from the Patterns menu.

The Pattern property can be used with the Set command to change
the selected pattern when drawing. The Patterns menu palette
(shown in Figure 4.4) contains the 40 different patterns arranged in
four columns of ten patterns each. Pattern 1 is in the upper left corner, pattern 10 is in the lower left corner, and pattern 40 is in the
lower right corner. To select a new pattern, enter the number of
the desired pattern as part of the Set command argument.

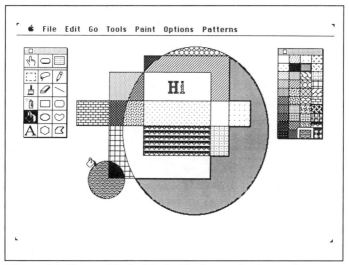

***Figure 4.4: Shapes filled with the Bucket tool using various
patterns***

EXAMPLES

get pattern

set the pattern to 5

set pattern to 25

PolySides

Sets the number of sides drawn by the Regular Polygon tool.

USAGE

The PolySides property can be used to select a new figure to be drawn with the Regular Polygon tool. You can change the figure by using the Set command with the PolySides property followed by a number over 3. The number used represents the number of sides in the regular polygon, except in the case of the circle. Three (the default) is used to create a triangle, 4 for a square, 5 for a pentagon, 6 for an hexagon, and 8 for an octagon. The higher the number, the more sides the polygon will have, and the more it will resemble a circle. An optimum number for creating a circle is about 50.

EXAMPLES

get the polySides

set the polySides to 4

set the polySides to 6

set polySides to 10

TextAlign

Sets the alignment of the paint text, text entered in fields, or the button name.

USAGE

You can use the TextAlign property to control the alignment of paint text as it is typed on the screen from the flashing text insertion pointer. To select a new alignment, use the Set command with the TextAlign property followed by left, right, or centered. The default setting for the program is left alignment.

Changing the text alignment with the TextAlign property and the Set command affects not only the alignment of paint text, but also text entered in the fields of the card and that of the button name when the ShowName button property is set to true.

EXAMPLES

get the textAlign

set the textAlign to centered

set textAlign to right

set the textAlign to left

TextFont

Sets the font of the paint text, text entered in fields, or the button name.

USAGE

You can use the TextFont property to set a new font for the paint text entered on the screen. To select a new font, you use the Set command with the TextFont property followed by the name of the font. Typical font choices include Chicago, Courier, Geneva, Helvetica, Monaco, New York, and Times.

Changing the font with the TextFont property and the Set command affects not only the font of paint text, but also text entered in the fields of the card and that of the button name when the ShowName button property is set to true.

EXAMPLES

get the textFont

set textFont to Chicago

set textFont to New York

set the textFont to Monaco

TextHeight

Sets the spacing (leading) between text that is entered with the Paint Text tool, entered in fields, or used for the button name.

USAGE

The TextHeight property can be used to control the amount of space between lines of text entered with the Paint Text tool. To set a new spacing (leading), you use the Set command with the TextHeight property followed by a number representing the number of points between the lines.

Changing the line spacing with the TextHeight property and the Set command affects not only the line spacing of paint text, but also that of fields in the card and the button name when the ShowName button property is set to true.

EXAMPLES

get the textHeight

set textHeight to 16

set the textHeight to 18

TextSize

Sets the size of the font of paint text, text entered in fields, or the button name.

You can use the TextSize property to control the size of the font when adding text with the Paint Text tool. To select a new font size, you use the Set command with the TextSize property followed by a number representing the point size of the font. The choice of font sizes varies according to the font specified by the TextFont property or selected from the Text Style dialog box, using the Text Style option on the Edit menu.

Changing the font size with the TextSize property and the Set command affects not only the size of paint text, but also that of text entered into fields in the card and that of the button name when the ShowName button property is set to true.

get the textSize

set the textSize to 10

set textSize to 18

set the textFont to Geneva
set the textSize to 20
set the textHeight to 24

TextStyle

Sets the style of the paint text, text entered in fields, or the button name.

USAGE

You can use the TextStyle property to assign special text enhancements such as bold, italic, or condensed lettering to text entered with the Paint Text tool. To select a new enhancement in a script, use the Set command with the TextStyle property followed by the name of the enhancement. The enhancements available include bold, italic, underline, outline, shadow, condense, extend, and plain. You can set more than one style at a time by separating the entries with commas.

Changing the text style with the TextStyle property and the Set command affects not only the style of paint text, but also that of text entered into fields in the card and that of the button name when the ShowName button property is set to true.

EXAMPLES

get the textStyle

set the textStyle to bold

set the textStyle to outline, shadow, extend

set textStyle to condense

set textStyle to plain

WINDOW PROPERTIES

There are three windows in HyperCard: the tool window (the Tools menu), the pattern window (the Patterns menu), and the message window (the Message box). There are three window properties that affect the use of these windows.

Location (Loc)

Changes the location of one of the HyperCard windows on the screen.

USAGE

The Location (or Loc) window property can be used to return the current location of the upper left corner of a HyperCard window or to set a new location for it. When used with the Set command to move the window, you specify the number of the horizontal and vertical screen coordinates for the upper left window corner, separated by commas. Note that you can use the Rectangle window property to get the current location of both the upper left and lower right corners of any of the three HyperCard windows.

EXAMPLES

```
get the loc of tool window
set the loc of message window to 30,250
set the location of pattern window to 225,100
```

SEE ALSO

Rectangle (window) property

Rectangle (Rect)

Gets the location of the upper left and lower right corner of the window.

USAGE

The Rectangle (or Rect) property is used with the Get command to return the horizontal and vertical coordinates of the top left and bottom right corners of the HyperCard window. The window coordinates are given as a list of coordinate numbers separated by commas in the order top left h,v and bottom right h,v. The Rectangle window property cannot be used with the Set command to change the size of any of the three HyperCard windows. Use the Location window property to change the position of the window on the screen.

EXAMPLES

   get the rect of message window

   get rect of tool window

   get the rectangle of pattern window

SEE ALSO

   Location (window) property

Visible

Controls whether the HyperCard window is displayed on the screen.

USAGE

When the Visible property is set to true, the HyperCard window is displayed on the screen. When the Visible property is set to false, the window is hidden from view. This can be used to remove the window from the screen or redisplay it. Note that you can also hide and redisplay the HyperCard windows using the Show and Hide Hyper-Talk commands.

EXAMPLES

get the visible of the message window

set visible of the tool window to true

set the visible of the pattern window to false

SEE ALSO

Hide command: Chapter 2
Show command: Chapter 2

STACK PROPERTIES

The stack properties are FreeSize, Name, Script, and Size. The FreeSize and Size properties cannot be changed with the Set command.

FreeSize

Describes the amount of space freed up in the stack by the deletion of objects such as buttons, fields, and cards from the stack.

USAGE

The FreeSize property cannot be changed with the Set command. When used with the Get command, it returns the number of unused (or free) bytes in the stack. Free space in the stack is unusable and can be removed only by the use of the Compact Stack option on the File menu when the user level is set to at least the Painting level.

EXAMPLE

See Figure 4.5.

```
on mouseUp
     get the freeSize of this stack
     if it > 500 then
          get the userLevel
          put it into tempLevel
          if tempLevel <= 2 then
               set the userLevel to 3
          end if
          doMenu "Compact Stack"
          set userLevel to tempLevel
     end if
end mouseUp
```

Figure 4.5: Example using FreeSize property

Name

Returns or changes the name of the stack.

You can use the Name property with the Set command to assign a new name to the stack. You can also use the Get command to return the current name of the stack. If you specify the *short name*, Hyper-Card returns only the name of the stack. If you specify *name* or *long name*, the program returns the word *stack* plus its name enclosed in quotation marks.

get name of stack – – stack "Home"

get short name of stack – – Home

set name of stack to "New History"

Name (background and card) property
Name (field) property
Name (button) property

Script

Returns or sets the script of a stack.

You can place the text of the script of a stack into the *it* variable by using the Script property with the Get command. You can also modify the script of any stack by using this property with the Set command.

get the script of this stack

get script of stack "Address"

set the script of stack "Wineries" to empty

set script of stack "Wineries" to card field "Script Editor"

where this field contains the message handler and HyperTalk commands for the new script for this stack.

Script (background and card) property
Script (field) property
Script (button) property

Size

Describes the current size in bytes of a stack.

USAGE

The size of a stack can be returned by using the Size property with the Get command. Naturally, it cannot be changed with the Set command.

EXAMPLES

get the size of this stack
get size of stack "Home"

BACKGROUND AND CARD PROPERTIES

The background and the card share the same properties, and therefore they are listed together in this section. These properties are the ID, Name, Number, and Script.

ID

Describes the ID number assigned to a background or card in the stack.

USAGE

ID numbers are assigned to backgrounds and cards as they are added to a stack. Once an ID number is assigned to a HyperCard object, it cannot be changed. Therefore, you cannot use the Set command to change this property. Only when the object is deleted is the ID number retired from use in the stack. You can use the Get command to return the ID number for any background or card in a stack (as well as fields and buttons; see the Field Properties and Button Properties sections).

EXAMPLES

   get the id of this stack

   get id of card "Marin"

   get the id of background

SEE ALSO

ID (field) property
ID (button) property

Name

Returns or changes the name of the background or card.

You can use the Name property with the Set command to assign a new name to a background or card. You can also use the Get command to return the current name of either of these objects. When you specify the *short name*, HyperCard returns only the name of the object. If you specify *name* or *long name*, the program returns the type of object, its ID number, and its name enclosed in quotation marks.

get name of card – – card "Home"

get short name of card – – Home

set the name of this card to "Inverness History"

get the name of this background

Name (stack) property
Name (field) property
Name (button) property

Number

Describes the number assigned to a background or card in the stack.

USAGE

The Number property can be used with the Get command to return the number assigned to either the background or card in a stack (stacks are not assigned numbers—only names). You cannot, however, change the background or card number with the Set command. These numbers are reassigned only when a background or object is deleted from the stack.

EXAMPLES

get the number of this card

get number of background id 3001

SEE ALSO

Number (field) property
Number (button) property

Script

Returns or sets the script of a background or card.

You can place the text of the script of a background or card into the *it* variable by using the Script property with the Get command. You can also modify the script of either of these objects by using this property with the Set command.

get the script of this background

get script of card 3

set the script of background 1 to empty

set script of background 1 to card field "Script Editor"

where this field contains the message handler and HyperTalk commands for the new script for this background.

Script (stack) property
Script (field) property
Script (button) property

FIELD PROPERTIES

The field properties apply to both the background and card fields in a stack. When retrieving or setting the property of a card field, you must use the word *card* when referring to that field. When you just enter *field*, the program assumes that you are referring to a background field.

ID

Returns the ID number of the field.

USAGE

You can use the Get command with the ID property to return the ID number assigned to a particular field. The ID number, however, cannot be changed with the Set command. The ID number assigned to a field is retired only when the field (or the card that the field is in) is deleted.

EXAMPLES

get the id of card field "Address"

get the id of field 5

Location (Loc)

Returns and sets the location of a field by the screen coordinates of its center.

USAGE

The Location (or Loc) property allows you to obtain or change the position of a particular field. When you use the field Location property with the Get command, the program returns the horizontal and vertical coordinates of the center point of the field. If you want to reposition the field in the card, enter the number of the horizontal and vertical screen coordinates, separated by a comma, as part of the Set command argument. Remember that these coordinates represent the center of the field, not the upper left corner (as when working with HyperCard windows).

EXAMPLES

get loc of card field 3

set the loc of field "Address" to 25,150

set the location of field 7 to 130,200

LockText

Controls whether the text of a field can be edited.

USAGE

The LockText property can be used to prevent a particular field from being edited. When the LockText property is set to true, the user cannot add, change, or delete text in the field. To unlock a field from a script, set the LockText property to false.

EXAMPLES

get the lockText of field 1

set lockText of field "Total" to true

set the lockText of card field "Comments" to false

Name

Returns or sets the name of the field.

You can use the Name property to obtain the name of a particular field or to assign a (new) name to a field. To assign a name to a field, use the Set command with the Name property and specify the field to be named by either ID or number. You can also get the short name—just the name without quotes—or the long name—containing the domain (card level), card ID number, stack name, and disk name —of a field.

get the name of field 2

set the name of card field 3 to "City"

set name of field id 4 to getName

where *getName* is a variable that contains the name to be given to this field.

Number

Returns the number of the field.

USAGE

Fields, both in the background and at the card level, are numbered by the program as they are created. You can use the Number property with the Get command in a script to return the number assigned to any field. You cannot, however, change the field number with the Set command. The only way to change a field number is to use the Bring Closer or Send Farther option on the HyperCard Objects menu.

EXAMPLES

get the number of field "State"

get number of card field 5

Rectangle (Rect)

Returns or sets the position of the field in the card.

USAGE

You can use the Rectangle (or Rect) property with the Get command to return the current position of a field given by the horizontal and vertical screen coordinates of its top left and bottom right corners. These coordinates are given in a list, with each coordinate number separated by a comma, that is placed in the *it* variable.

You can also use the Rectangle property to change the position and size of a field in the card from a script. When used with the Set command, you must list the new horizontal and vertical coordinates of both the upper left and lower right corners as part of the Set command argument. Note that if you specify corner coordinates that are beyond the HyperCard screen area (0,0 to 342,512), the field will not be visible until you move it within this area using another Set command with the Rectangle property.

Unlike the Location field property, which can be used only to reposition the field on the card, the Rectangle property can also be used to resize the field. This makes it possible to hide some, or all, of the information in the field by specifying a field size smaller than can accommodate all of the information that the field contains.

EXAMPLES

get rect of field "State"

get the rectangle of card field 2

set rect of field 4 to 174,117,323,157

SEE ALSO

Location (field) property

Script

Returns or sets the script of a field.

USAGE

You can place the text of the script of a field into the *it* variable by using the Script property with the Get command. You can also modify the script of any one of these objects by using this property with the Set command.

EXAMPLES

get the script of field "Total"

set script of field 2 to empty

set the script of field 2 to card field 1

where *card field 1* contains the new message handler and HyperTalk commands for field 2.

Scroll

Sets the number of pixels that the program scrolls the text in a scrolling field.

USAGE

The Scroll property can be used only with fields assigned the scrolling type to obtain or set how far down the text of the field is to scroll. The amount of scrolling is measured by the number of pixels from the top of the text in the field. To determine how many lines a particular number of pixels advances the text of a field, you divide the number of pixels by the line height (the leading) of the field.

The Scroll property can be used to advance to a particular line of text in a scrolling field when viewing from the first line of text is not desirable. You can save a result obtained by the Scroll property and use it to advance to the same position in related scrolling fields in other cards of the stack.

EXAMPLES

set the scroll of field 1 to 50
set scroll of card field "Comments" to scrollPixels

where *scrollPixels* is a local variable.

ShowLines

Controls whether the lines of a text field are visible on the screen.

USAGE

The line separators of a HyperCard field can be made visible or invisible on the screen, as you see fit. To obtain the current setting for a particular field, you use the ShowLines property with the Get command. To change the setting, you use this property with the Set command. When the ShowLines property is set to true, the lines of the field are visible on the screen. When the ShowLines property is set to false, they are invisible.

EXAMPLES

get the showLines of field "Address"

set showLines of field 3 to true

set the showLines of card field 10 to false

Style

Returns or sets the style of a field.

USAGE

When you create a new field, you have the opportunity to select among several different field styles. If you do not select a new style, the default field style assigned by the program is transparent. You can use the Style property with the Get command to obtain the current style of any field. Moreover, you can change the style of a field by using the Style property with the Set command and entering the style name as part of the command argument. The style names are transparent, opaque, rectangle, shadow, and scrolling. This property is often used with scripts that create new fields in a card to select a field style other than transparent.

EXAMPLES

get the style of field "City"

set style of field 4 to scrolling

set the style of card field 1 to transparent

set style of field id 20 to shadow

TextAlign

See TextAlign under Paint Properties

TextFont

See TextFont under Paint Properties

TextHeight

See TextHeight under Paint Properties

TextSize

See TextSize under Paint Properties

TextStyle

See TextStyle under Paint Properties

Visible

Controls whether the field is visible in the card.

USAGE

When the Visible property is set to true for a field, its information is visible on the screen. If a style other than transparent is used, you can see its outline as well. If the ShowLines property is set to true, you can also see the number of text lines. To hide a field from a script, you can use the Set command with the Visible property and set it to false. The Visible property provides an alternate method to using the Hide and Show commands in a script to hide and then redisplay a field in a card.

EXAMPLES

get the visible of field 8

set visible of card field "Notes" to false

set the visible of field id 5 to true

SEE ALSO

Hide command: Chapter 2
Show command: Chapter 2

WideMargins

Controls whether the field uses wide margins.

USAGE

When you create a field, you can specify that it use wide margins, which increase the space allotted to both the left and right margins, thus allowing less text to be entered on each line than when using the standard margins in a field. With the WideMargins property, you turn on or off these wide margins in a particular field. To turn on wide margins, set the WideMargins property to true. To turn off wide margins, set it to false. You can also obtain the current setting of this field attribute (returned as either true or false in the *it* variable) by using the property as the argument of the Get command.

EXAMPLES

get the wideMargins of field 5

set wideMargins of card field "Company" to true

set the wideMargins of field id 53 to false

BUTTON PROPERTIES

The button properties apply to both the background and card buttons in a stack. When retrieving or setting the property of a background button, you must use the word *bkgnd* when referring to that button. When you just enter *button*, the program assumes that you are referring to a card button. Note that this is just the opposite of the way HyperCard refers to background and card fields in a stack.

AutoHilite

Controls whether a button is briefly highlighted when it is clicked.

USAGE

When the AutoHilite property is set to true, the button is momentarily highlighted when the user clicks on it, as long as the style of the button is not the check box or radio button (auto highlighting does not work with these types of buttons). When the AutoHilite property is set to false, this highlighting does not take place when the button is clicked. You can also use this property with the Get command to obtain the current status of the auto highlighting feature for a particular button.

EXAMPLES

    get the autoHilite of bkgnd button 3
    set autoHilite of button "OK" to true
    set the autoHilite of bkgnd button 4 to false

Hilite

Controls whether a button is highlighted.

USAGE

When the Hilite property is set to true, the button appears highlighted. If the style of the button is anything other than the check box or radio button style and the button shows its name, highlighting makes the button name appear reversed (in white letters on a black background rather than the standard black on white). When the check box or radio button style is highlighted, the button is selected with a check mark in the case of the check box or a dot in the case of the radio button. Highlighting is used to show which button is the default choice when several buttons offer different alternatives.

As well as being able to turn on highlighting for a button with the Hilite property, you can also use it to turn off highlighting (with the Set command) or to obtain the current status of highlighting for a button (with the Get command).

EXAMPLES

get the hilite of bkgnd button 2

set the hilite of bkgnd button 5 to false

set hilite of button "New Card" to true

Icon

Controls the icon used with a button.

You can use the Icon property to return or set an icon to be associated with a particular button. When you use the Icon property to obtain the icon used with a particular button, the program returns the number of the icon assigned to the button (if any). When you use the Icon property with the Set command to assign a new icon to a button, you can refer to the icon either by number or by name. When referring to the icon name, be sure to enclose it in a pair of quotation marks when the button name includes a space. To remove an icon from a button, enter 0 as the icon number in the Set command.

To view the available icons, select a button and then click on the Icon button in the Button Information dialog box. This will bring you to a scroll box containing all of the icons. Each icon is identified by ID number and name when you select it. Icons are resources that you can copy to a stack by using a utility such as ResEdit. To be able to assign a new icon to a button, it must be available in the current stack, in the Home stack, or to HyperCard itself.

get the icon of bkgnd button 1

set icon of button "MacWrite" to "MacWrite"

set icon of bkgnd button 5 to 1008

ID

Returns the ID number of the button.

USAGE

You can use the Get command with the ID property to return the ID number assigned to a particular button. The ID number, however, cannot be changed with the Set command. The ID number assigned to a button is retired only when the button (or the card that the button is in) is deleted.

EXAMPLES

get the id of button 5

get the id of bkgnd button 5

get the id of button "Next"

Location (Loc)

Returns and sets the location of a button by the screen coordinates of its center.

USAGE

The Location (or Loc) property allows you to obtain or change the position of a particular button. When you use the button Location property with the Get command, the program returns the horizontal and vertical coordinates of the center point of the button. If you want to reposition the button in the card, enter the number of the horizontal and vertical screen coordinates, separated by a comma, as part of the Set command argument. Remember that these coordinates represent the center of the button, not the upper left corner (as when working with HyperCard windows).

EXAMPLES

get the loc of bkgnd button id 4567

set the location of button 3 to 320,175

set loc of bkgnd button "Prev" to 250,330

Name

Returns or sets the name of the button.

USAGE

You can use the Name property to obtain the name of a particular button or to assign a (new) name to a button. To assign a name to a button, use the Set command with the Name property and specify the button to be named by either ID or number. You can also get the short name and the long name of a button. The short name is just the name without quotes. The long name contains the domain (background level), card ID number, stack name, and disk name.

EXAMPLES

get the name of bkgnd button 3

set the name of button 5 to "Next"

set name of bkgnd button 16 to "Home"

Number

Returns the number of a button.

Buttons, both in the background and at the card level, are numbered by the program as they are created. You can use the Number property with the Get command in a script to return the number assigned to any button. You cannot, however, change the button number with the Set command. The only way to change a button number is to use the Bring Closer or Send Farther option on the HyperCard Objects menu.

get the number of bkgnd button "Home"

get number of button "Sum"

get the number of button id 67

Rectangle (Rect)

Returns or sets the position of the button in the card.

You can use the Rectangle (or Rect) property with the Get command to return the current position of a button given by the horizontal and vertical screen coordinates of its top left and bottom right corners. These coordinates are given in a list, with each coordinate number separated by a comma, that is placed in the *it* variable.

You can also use the Rectangle property to change the position and size of a button in the card from a script. When using this property with the Set command, you must list the new horizontal and vertical coordinates of both the upper left and lower right corners as part of the Set command argument. Note that if you specify corner coordinates that are beyond the HyperCard screen area (0,0 to 342,512), the button will not be visible until you move it within this area by using another Set command with the Rectangle property.

Unlike the Location button property, which can be used only to reposition the button on the card, the Rectangle property can also be used to resize the button. This makes it possible to hide the entire button or just its icon and/or name (if the ShowName property is set to true) by specifying a button size smaller than can display this information.

get the rectangle of bkgnd button 3

set rect of button "Comments" to 20,250,27,280

Location (button) property

Script

Returns or sets the button script.

You can place the text of the script of a button into the *it* variable by using the Script property with the Get command. You can also modify the script of a button by using this property with the Set command.

get the script of button 12

set script of bkgnd button 1 to empty

set script of bkgnd button 1 to card field 2

where *card field 2* contains the message handler and HyperTalk commands for the new button script.

ShowName

Controls whether the button name is displayed.

If you set the ShowName property to true, the name assigned to the button (either at creation or with the Name property) is displayed in the button. If you set the ShowName property to true, the name is not displayed. You can also use the ShowName property with the Get command, which returns either true or false, to check the current status of the ShowName property for a particular button.

get the showName of bkgnd button 9

set showName of bkgnd button "More" to true

set the showName of button "More Buttons" to false

Style

Controls the style of the button.

USAGE

When you create a new button, you have the opportunity to select among several different button styles. If you do not select a new style, the default button style assigned by the program is a round rectangle. You can use the Style property with the Get command to obtain the current style of any button. In addition, you can change the style of a button by using the Style property with the Set command and entering the style name as part of the command argument. The style names are transparent, opaque, rectangle, shadow, round-Rect, checkBox, and radioButton.

EXAMPLES

get the style of bkgnd button id 34

set the style of bkgnd button "Home" to opaque

set style of button 2 to transparent

set style of bkgnd button 3 to radioButton

TextAlign

See TextAlign under Paint Properties

TextFont

See TextFont under Paint Properties

TextHeight

See TextHeight under Paint Properties

TextSize

See TextSize under Paint Properties

TextStyle

See TextStyle under Paint Properties

Visible

Controls whether the button is visible on the screen.

USAGE

When the Visible property is set to true for a button, its outline, icon, and name are visible on the screen (provided that its style shows the outline of the button, an icon has been assigned, and the ShowName property is set to true). To hide a button from a script, you can use the Set command with the Visible property and set it to false. The Visible property provides an alternate method to using the Hide and Show commands in a script to hide and then redisplay a button in a card.

EXAMPLES

get the visible of bkgnd button id 230

set the visible of bkgnd button "Hidden" to true

set visible of button 3 to false

SEE ALSO

Hide command: Chapter 2
Show command: Chapter 2

CHAPTER 5

Constants in HyperTalk

HyperTalk includes several constants that are used in scripts either when testing for a particular condition or to enter characters such as the quote, return, tab, or space (without having to refer to their ASCII code numbers) or a value such as π. Constants, as their name implies, are the opposite of variables because their values are always the same regardless of how they are used in scripts.

Down

A condition returned by the ShiftKey, OptionKey, CommandKey, and Mouse functions to indicate that the key is depressed.

USAGE

Most often, you will use the ShiftKey, OptionKey, CommandKey, or Mouse function as part of If...Then constructions, which test if the particular key (or mouse button) is depressed when the message handler containing the function is executed. You can test for the Down or Up constant as part of the If...Then expression (see the examples in the following section).

EXAMPLES

if shiftKey is down then exit mouseUp

if the commandKey is down then go to stack "Help"

if the mouse is down then go home

SEE ALSO

Up constant

Empty

The null string, which is the same as " ".

The Empty constant has two uses in HyperTalk scripts. You can use it to clear out the contents of a particular HyperCard container such as a field or variable. You can also use it as part of an If...Then expression to test whether a particular container is empty.

```
put empty into field 1  - - clears out current contents

on mouseUp
   if field "Name" is empty then
      ask "What is your name?"
      put it into field "Name"
   end if
end mouseUp
```

False

Used to set up a flag that stores false to a variable that is tested later in the script.

USAGE

The True and False constants are naturally returned by all conditional constructions set up in HyperTalk scripts. However, the use of the True and False constants is not required within the construction because they are implied by the nature of the condition (when the condition *if field 1 is empty then...* is evaluated, it is either true because field 1 is indeed empty or false because it contains some data).

However, the True and False constants are useful in scripts where you want to set up a flag by initializing a variable with either one of them. After setting up a flag, you can then use it as part of the test in an If...Then construction or as part of the argument of a Repeat construction (see the example in the following section).

EXAMPLE

```
set testVar to false  - -  testVar is a local variable
.
.
.
repeat while testVar  - -  same as test while false
```

SEE ALSO

True constant

FormFeed

The form-feed character—ASCII code 12.

The form-feed character sent by the FormFeed constant (ASCII code 12) instructs the printer to advance to the next top-of-form, as marked by the printer. This constant can be used when exporting data from a HyperCard stack to a text file with the Write command to include the form-feed character as part of the new text file.

```
open file "Johnson Text"
write field 1 to "Johnson Text"
write formFeed to file "Johnson Text"
close file "Johnson Text"

charToNum(formFeed)  - - returns 12
```

LineFeed

The line-feed character—ASCII code 10.

The line-feed character sent by the LineFeed constant (ASCII code 10) sends a carriage return and an "advance to the beginning of the next line" command to the printer or telecommuncations device. It can be used when exporting data from a HyperCard stack to a text file with the Write command to include the line-feed character in the new text file.

```
open file "Stock Quotes"
write field 2 to "Stock Quotes"
write return & lineFeed to field "Stock Quotes"
write field 3 to "Stock Quotes"
close file "Stock Quotes"

charToNum(lineFeed)  – –  returns 10
```

Quote

The double quotation mark character (″).

USAGE

Because the double quotation mark is used to delimit text in Hyper-Talk statements, you use the Quote constant when you want to include the quotation mark within a text string. You cannot add this character to a text string by enclosing it within another pair of quotation marks, since HyperCard interprets any quotation mark as either the beginning or end of a character string. Note from the example in the following section that the Quote constant is joined to the standard delimited text by the **&** (ampersand), the concatenation operator in HyperCard.

EXAMPLE

put "She says," & quote & "Never!" & quote into field 1

Thus, field 1 contains the text *She says, "Never!"*

Pi

The mathematical constant π.

USAGE

The Pi constant substitutes the value

3.14159265358979323846

in any HyperTalk statement. This is the approximate value of the ratio of the circumference of a circle to its diameter. It is much easier (and safer) to use the Pi constant in computations that require the use of this ratio (as with the trigonometric functions) than it is to enter the approximate value with its 20 decimal places.

EXAMPLES

```
put (pi*field 1) ^ 2 into field "Circle Area"
put sin(47.5*pi/180) into AngleC
```

where *AngleC* is a local variable.

Return

The carriage-return character—ASCII code 13.

USAGE

The carriage return (ASCII code 13) produced by using the Return constant signifies the end of a line in a text field or the end of a programming statement in the Script Editor. The carriage-return character is entered from the keyboard by pressing the Return key (or sometimes the Enter key). To enter a carriage return from a HyperTalk script, you use the Return constant. Most often, you will use this constant when importing and exporting data to and from HyperCard. It is most useful when importing data from a word processing field into a HyperCard field with the Read command, where it is used as the delimiting character.

EXAMPLES

```
on mouseUp
  open file readFrom  - - readFrom is a variable name
  read from file readFrom until return
  close file readFrom
end mouseUp

charToNum(return)  - - returns 13
```

SEE ALSO

Read command: Chapter 2
Write command: Chapter 2

Space

The space character—ASCII code 32.

USAGE

The space character (ASCII code 32) produced by the Space constant can be entered from the keyboard into any HyperTalk script simply by pressing the Space bar. Therefore, this constant is mostly used with the Put command to add spaces between text components using the appropriate chunk expression.

EXAMPLES

charToNum(space) – – returns 32

put space before word 3 of field 2

put space & space after word 2 of field 7

This places two spaces between the second and third words in field 7.

SEE ALSO

Put command: Chapter 2

TAB **313**

Tab

The tab character—ASCII code 9.

The tab character (ASCII code 9) produced by the Tab constant signifies the end of text field in HyperCard. In other Macintosh applications such as spreadsheets and database managers, the tab
character also signifies the end of a basic component (*cell* in a spreadsheet, or *field* in a database). Most often, the Tab character is used in
importing and exporting data to and from HyperCard. It is especially useful when importing data into a HyperCard field from a
spreadsheet or database program where the Tab constant is used as
the delimiting character.

```
on mouseUp
  open file readFrom  -- readFrom is a variable name
  read from file readFrom until tab
  close file readFrom
end mouseUp

charToNum(tab)  -- returns 9
```

Read command: Chapter 2
Write command: Chapter 2

True

Used to set up a flag that stores true to a variable that is tested later in the script.

USAGE

The usage of the True constant is similar to that of the False constant (although they are opposite in meaning). See the Usage section of the False constant for information on how they are both used in HyperTalk.

EXAMPLE

```
set testVar to true  -- testVar is a local variable
.
.
.
if testVar is false then beep 2
```

SEE ALSO

False constant

Up

A condition returned by the ShiftKey, OptionKey, CommandKey, and Mouse functions to indicate that they are not depressed.

USAGE

The usage of the Up constant with the ShiftKey, OptionKey, CommandKey, and Mouse functions is similar to that of Down constant (although opposite in meaning). See the Down constant for more information on usage.

EXAMPLES

if shiftKey is up then exit mouseUp

if the commandKey is up then go to stack "Help"

if the mouse is up then beep 3

SEE ALSO

Down constant

Zero to Ten

The same as entering the the numbers 0 to 10 in a script.

USAGE

HyperCard understands the use of the words *zero, one, two, three,...ten* in scripts as though you had entered the equivalent digits 0, 1, 2, 3,...10. If you want to enter the word *zero* into a HyperCard container rather than the digit *0,* be sure to enclose it in quotation marks, as in

put "zero" into field "Name"

EXAMPLES

Put zero into card field 3   – –   field 3 contains 0

Put nine * two into newNumber

where *newNumber* is a local variable, containing the product 18.